Twenty Affordable Sailboats

To Take You Anywhere

by

Gregg Nestor

Paradise Cay Publications, Inc
Arcata, California

Cover design by Rob Johnson, www.johnsondesign.org
Editing and book design by Linda Morehouse, www.WeBuildBooks.com

Printed in the United States
First Edition
ISBN 0-939837-72-2, 978-0-939837-72-2

Published by Paradise Cay Publications, Inc.
P. O. Box 29
Arcata, CA 95518-0029
800-736-4509
707-822-9163 Fax
paracay@humboldt1.com
www.paracay.com

This book is dedicated to sailing couples everywhere
who are planning to live their dream of cruising the world
and to those who are considering it.

CONTENTS

Acknowledgments

I would like to take this opportunity to acknowledge the many sailors and non-sailors alike who helped to make this book possible. Many are quoted within the following pages, but there are many others who are not mentioned individually. My sincere appreciation to all of you. Specifically, I would like to thank Karen Larson, whose faith in me and whose encouragement helped this book come to fruition.

FOREWORD

To explain the genesis of this book we have to go back a few years to when I wrote *Twenty Small Sailboats to Take You Anywhere.* Most of those boats were truly small, the kind I like best. They were also inexpensive and ideally suited to young bravehearts more interested in seeing the world on a shoestring than living aboard a floating condo with all the luxuries of home.

Now, I can say this until I'm blue in the face: Small boats are not necessarily less seaworthy than big boats, but the general perception, certainly in North America, is that bigger is safer and better.

Thus, I began to receive letters and e-mails from people wanting a book featuring bigger, more comfortable boats. Perhaps people are better off these days, more affluent. Perhaps they just have better access to credit. Even felons in prison joined the chorus. You'd hardly believe how many felons wrote to me, urging me to raise my sights, fer chrissake.

North Americans are also acutely aware of outward appearance, of style, and I have to agree that a 25-foot sailboat is not likely to generate a satisfactory degree of envy in your neighbor unless you coat the decks with gold leaf.

So Gregg Nestor has bravely stepped in to fill the vacuum. Here you are then, twenty bigger boats that will take you across as many oceans as you like, with greater comfort, more style, and more people.

Gregg has done a fine research job here, one pleasingly devoid of flimflam. It's a truly helpful tool for those of you wading with trepidation into the murky waters of boat-buying. I wish it every success, and I hope all you affluent felons will get off my back now and write to Gregg instead.

—John Vigor

PREFACE

If you're shopping for an affordable sailboat that you can own for years to come, Gregg Nestor has just done you a big favor. He has written the book you're looking for: *Twenty Affordable Sailboats to Take You Anywhere*. Sound familiar? It might, because this book follows John Vigor's very popular book, Twenty Small Sailboats to Take You Anywhere. Both books have been published by Paradise Cay Publications, Inc.

Gregg, who writes many of the boat reviews for *Good Old Boat* magazine, was a natural author for this book. On behalf of this magazine, he has acquired a great deal of experience crawling in and out of cubbyholes on many sailboats. He is as unbiased as any sailor can be about something as opinion-provoking as a cruising sailboat. His selection of twenty boats is as good as it gets.

As he does with his reviews for *Good Old Boat,* Gregg researches the boat designer and the manufacturer and gives his readers not only the highlights of the boat but also the highlights of its birth back in the 1960s, 1970s, or 1980s. This is, by the way, how one finds an affordable boat: One reaches back into a previous era and finds a gem that has already stood the test of time. Call it a classic fiberglass yacht. Call it a good old boat. Whatever you call it, this boat is part of the affordable dream.

Naturally the majority of effort for each boat is spent on a review of its design and sailing characteristics. But Gregg goes beyond all that with insightful comments by an owner or two, a note about what you might expect to pay for a boat of this kind today, specific weaknesses to check out if you've already fallen in love with a particular boat, specifications for the boat, sailplan and accommodation plan drawings, owners' groups that will help you find others who sail and love boats like this, and the important comparative calculations that matter.

Speaking of these comparative calculations, Gregg takes a page to explain each. This is a question that comes up time and time again in the world of boat reviews. And he offers a spreadsheet comparing the twenty boats he's selected: specifications and calculations. There's a helpful bibliography also.

Gregg has created a useful, thorough, and helpful book if you're in the market for an affordable sailboat capable of taking you coastal hopping or well beyond your home waters. You'll find this book to be interesting reading even if you're not currently prowling the dockyards and marinas for your next boat.

—Karen Larson, *Good Old Boat* Magazine

Introduction

In the pages that follow, you will find in-depth reviews of twenty affordable, comfortable, and seaworthy sailboats. None of them is brand new, nor is any antique. All were once prominent offerings during that somewhat golden double decade of fiberglass sailboats, the '70s and '80s. All were designed by some of the world's leading naval architects and produced by reputable manufacturers.

Each sailboat has its own chapter, in which you will find detailed information on design and construction, accommodations, handling characteristics, things to check out, and price and availability. For ease of comparison, there's a spreadsheet—located in Appendix C—containing the numerical values for all the boats.

Selection for inclusion into this group of twenty sailboats was based on the following criteria:

Modest Price: Affordability is the key word here. Prices for these boats range from $20,000 to $70,000 on the used boat market. Knowing that upgrades and refitting may add close to an additional 50 percent of the purchase cost, this still keeps the total cost of each boat below that magic $100,000 number.

Availability: None of these boats is difficult to find, rare, one-of-a-kind, or even the result of a very short production run. All are available in North America.

Comfort: While size is generally a major factor, using it along with the combination of ratios found in Appendix A minimizes subjectivity and yields a more empirical approach.

Practical Size: These sailboats range from 30 to 38 feet in length and have a minimum beam of 10 feet. The boats are sized for a cruising couple, but are big enough to accommodate an occasional cruising hitchhiker or two.

Seaworthiness: All of these boats have crossed oceans and will take you around the world.

Above Average Safety: Consideration is given to the combination of each boat's historical safety performance, its capsize screening factor ratio, and the other ratios listed under Comfort.

This book is by no means an exhaustive list of all affordable, comfortable, and seaworthy sailboats, but rather is a representative selection of twenty whose design and construction are suited for serious offshore sailing.

If you are leaning towards taking one of these boats to do some serious offshore sailing, there is a caveat: You should go through the boat from stem to stern, replacing gear that is tired or suspect, repairing as necessary and reinforcing where needed. Also, nothing takes the place of a thorough professional survey, and nothing—I mean nothing—replaces good seamanship. It's common sense. Bon voyage.

“If a man must be obsessed by something,
I suppose a boat is as good as anything,
perhaps a bit better than most.
A small sailing craft is not only beautiful,
it is seductive and full of strange promise and the hint of trouble.”

E.B. White, *The Sea and the Wind that Blows* 1977

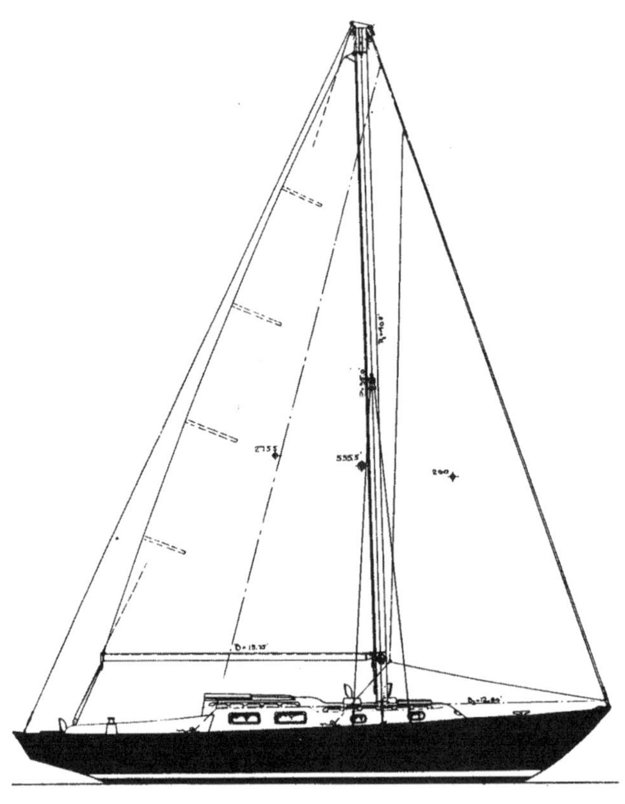

ALBERG 35

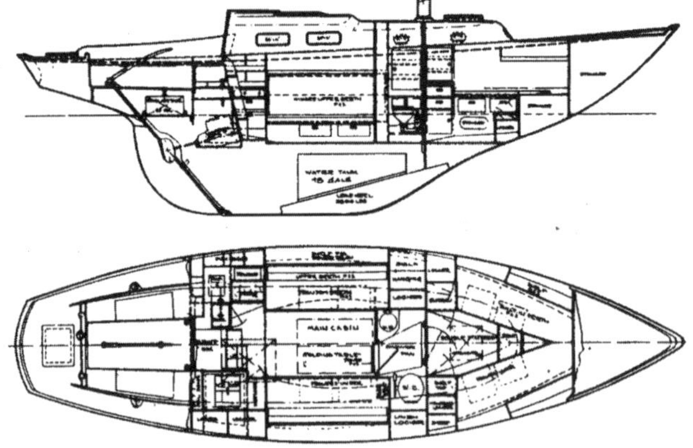

ALBERG 35

A classic ocean cruiser with a proven pedigree.

Carl Arne Alberg was born on April 11, 1901 in Gothenburg, Sweden. As a young boy, he was interested in yacht design and even wrote of the difficulties of choosing the perfect bow design. Carl went on to pursue his interest at the Chalmers Institute of Technology in Gothenburg, where he studied naval architecture and marine engineering.

By the mid-1920s Carl had emigrated to the United States. He first worked as a rigger, then became a master shipwright, and soon thereafter was hired by John Alden as a designer. While at the John Alden Company, Carl concentrated on designs that expressed seaworthiness, comfort, and boats that would sail on their bottoms.

In 1946, Carl left the John Alden Company to hang out his own shingle. For about three years, he designed wooden boats. However, the combination of a business slowdown and the Korean War prompted Carl to accept employment with the U.S. Coast Guard; for 10 years he worked as their chief marine engineer/architect.

In 1958, Carl made the switch from wooden sailing yachts to fiberglass sailboats; Everett and Clint Pearson introduced his design for a 28-foot cruising sailboat at the New York Boat Show in January 1959. The boat was the Pearson Triton. The rest is history.

The Alberg 35 is but one of several classic cruising yachts designed by Carl Alberg and built by Pearson Yachts of Bristol, Rhode Island. Introduced in 1961, it was a fixture in the Pearson line until 1967. During its six-year production run, approximately 280 Alberg 35s were built. From both sales and performance viewpoints, the Alberg 35 was a very successful production yacht.

Although a bit long in the tooth, the Alberg 35 continues to deliver sailing pleasure and adventure, while demonstrating Carl Alberg's legacy of a well-designed, good-looking cruising boat that is both exciting and safe to sail, without the threat of an easy capsize. The Alberg 35's capsize screening ratio is 1.66, well below the magic 2.0, which is the maximum to be considered an acceptable blue-water candidate.

Design and Construction

All Alberg-designed boats have distinctive lines and shared characteristics. The Alberg 35 is no exception to this seaworthy Scandinavian influence. The boat exhibits a somewhat flat yet springy sheer; a spoon bow; long, balanced overhangs; a rounded cabin trunk; a slightly raised doghouse; winch pedestals; and wooden cockpit coamings, all hallmarks of Carl's.

The Alberg 35's design was a product of the CCA (Cruising Club of America) measurement rule and represented the state of the art racer/ cruiser for 1962. By today's standards, the beam is a bit narrow at 9 feet 8 inches, and the waterline at 24 feet is a tad short. These proportions are good for gliding along in light air, in spite of the boat's somewhat squatty rig. Add a breeze, and the boat's powerful ends help extend the waterline length when the hull heels. The boat's underbody displays a 5-foot 2-inch cutaway full keel and an attached rudder. With a displacement of 13,000 pounds, 5,300 pounds of that in the form of encapsulated lead ballast, the Alberg 35 affords a sea-kindly motion. It has a solid motion comfort ratio of 34.6.

Both the hull and deck of the Alberg 35 are of fiberglass construction. While the hull is a heavy, uncored hand laminate that has been found to be greater than one inch thick below the waterline, the deck is a sandwich of two layers of fiberglass with a core of balsa wood. Balsa is extremely light and, when sandwiched in this manner, adds structural rigidity. It also affords good insulation against heat, cold, and sound.

Unfortunately, the balsa used in many early fiberglass production boats was not end-grain, but rather edge-grain. A sandwich incorporating edge-grain balsa lacks the stiffness and the compression strength of an end-grain balsa sandwich. Fortunately, Everett Pearson pioneered the use of end-grain balsa as a coring material. However, constant flexing of cored decks can cause a break in the bond between the two fiberglass skins and the balsa core. Also, any water that might find its way beneath the fiberglass skin can turn the core into mush.

If the deck feels mushy beneath your feet or gives off a dull thud when struck with a mallet, it's a good bet that the deck is at least partially delaminated. While small areas of deck sponginess can be corrected, extensive delamination is reason enough to reject the boat.

The underbody of the Alberg 35 has a cutaway full keel with its 5,300 pounds of ballast fully encapsulated. The ballast is a single lead casting that was lowered into the hollow fiberglass keel molding and then glassed over. This encapsulated ballast eliminates the concern for corroded keel bolts since there aren't any. However, some boats have a void between the bottom of the lead casting and the fiberglass shell. This makes the fiberglass shell vulnerable to damage from groundings. Should a surveyor find that this condition exists, it can be corrected by filling the void with epoxy resin.

The rudder is tiller operated (wheel steering was an option) and attached to the keel on a raked rudder post. The rudder itself is wooden and the post a heavy bronze rod. While the design is dated, this form of construction is sound; it can be easily inspected and maintained and, best of all, upgraded.

ON DECK

With the exception of the port and starboard mooring cleats and a deck pipe leading to the chain locker, the foredeck is completely free of clutter, thus providing a good working platform from which to deploy or retrieve an anchor or make headsail changes. Located on top of the rounded cabin trunk is the teak-covered forward hatch. This hatch, along with a pair of bronze-framed opening ports, provides ventilation for the forward cabin. Located just aft of the mast is a pair of cowl vents attached to Dorade boxes, as well as another pair of opening ports. This combination affords light and ventilation to the head. The slightly raised doghouse outwardly denotes the main cabin, which is naturally illuminated by four fixed portlights. To assist in forward and aft on-deck movement, there are wide sidedecks, outboard shrouds, and four sections of teak handrail along the cabin's top.

The cockpit is long and large. There's plenty of room for daysailing and entertaining, but size is a concern when considering serious offshore work. The cockpit is self-draining and there is a bona fide bridge deck to prevent water from cascading below should a wave fill the cockpit. The teak cockpit coamings are relatively high and afford reasonable, but less than comfortable, back support. The standard tiller is long and takes up a lot of cockpit space. Pedestal wheel steering was available and many boats have been fitted with this option. There are large port and starboard cockpit seat lockers as well as a true lazarette, with its hatch located just aft of the mainsheet traveler. These stowage areas share three undesirable characteristics: inadequate water-tightness, poor fasteners, and draining that goes directly into the bilge. All of these conditions should be addressed before heading out for some serious blue-water sailing.

BELOW DECK

Just aft of the chain locker is a large forward cabin with a V-berth, a hanging locker, a bureau, four drawers beneath the berth, and fiddled shelves outboard and above. Because of the lack of an insert and the arrangement of the V-berth, there is adequate floor space and standing headroom to change clothes, rummage through lockers, and move about.

Abaft the forward cabin is the head compartment, which spans the full width of the boat. This provides for a fair amount of useable, maneuverable space. The head and a linen locker are to starboard, while the sink, a hanging locker, and additional stowage are to port. The shower is on the centerline and incorporates its own sump. The Alberg 35 was one of the first boats of this size to come standard with a shower and pressurized hot and cold water. Privacy is afforded the head by closing the doors to the forward cabin and main saloon.

The main saloon is offered in two configurations: number one is the "traditional" opposing settee arrangement, while number two is the more "modern" dinette arrangement. In configuration number one, the settees face each other and incorporate a bulkhead-mounted, drop leaf table between them. In this configuration, the galley is aft and spans the width of the boat. There are no quarter berths, and the settees would be used as sea berths. The aft galley incorporates a small sink and two-burner alcohol stove to port, a top-loading icebox to starboard. When closed, the icebox provides galley counter space and serves as a navigational chart table.

The number two dinette arrangement is characterized by a U-shaped dinette on the port side and the galley to starboard. This arrangement offers some interesting possibilities. First of all, if you lower the dining table, you can quickly convert the dinette to a double berth. Also, the galley is a bit more workable. There is room for a three-burner stove/oven along with the icebox, sink, and food lockers. Since the galley no longer spans the aft portion of the main saloon, there's room for two quarter berths. These extend beneath the cockpit seats and make for reasonable sea berths. As far as a chart table is concerned, the dining table will have to pull double duty.

Although the forward cabin and the head compartment achieve adequate ventilation though the use of either an overhead hatch or cowl vents, ventilation in the main saloon is severely lacking except for the main companionway hatch.

The interior décor is dated. Pearson finished the bulkheads, cabinetry, and so forth in what they termed "low maintenance" wood-grained plastic laminate. With a little sanding and painting of the laminate and varnishing of the standard teak trim, the boat's interior appearance will improve dramatically. Headroom is a generous 6 feet 4 inches.

The engine is situated beneath and behind the companionway stairs; by removing several panels, near total access can be obtained. Likewise, lifting the cabin sole provides access to the potable water tank and the relatively deep bilge.

Depending upon the production year, the Alberg 35 can be fitted with a variety of tankage, including materials of construction, location, and volume. The design specifications for a late production run boat call for an integral fiberglass 48-gallon potable water tank to be located in the bilge beneath the cabin sole, and a 23-gallon Monel fuel tank to be placed behind the engine and beneath the cockpit sole.

Specifications

LOA .... 34'9"
LWL .... 24'0"
Beam .... 9'8"
Draft .... 5'2"
Displacement .... 12,600 lbs.
Ballast .... 5,300 lbs.
Sail Area .... (sloop/yawl) 545/583 sq. ft.

THE RIG

The Alberg 35 is available in two configurations: a sloop and a yawl. The Cruising Club of America (CCA) rule lightly taxed the mizzen sail and permitted the mizzen staysail to be carried without any penalty. This rule made the yawl quite popular. The rig's mizzen can be used to help balance the boat. It is especially helpful in maneuvering in a crowded anchorage while under sail. Nevertheless, when one compares the actual performance of the yawl and the sloop, the sloop comes out ahead.

Both the sloop and the yawl use the same mast location. It is somewhat forward and therefore results in a small fore triangle and large low aspect ratio mainsail. One of the benefits of this rig is that the Alberg 35 can be sailed quite effectively under main alone. The sail area/displacement ratio is 16.1 for the sloop and 17.2 for the yawl.

The Alberg 35's mast height is 44 feet 6 inches from waterline to masthead. The mast is stepped on deck and supported below by a bridge and two compression posts. The mast standing rigging is comprised of a forestay, a single pair of cap shrouds, dual lower shrouds, a single pair of spreaders, and a backstay. The mast is anodized aluminum, while the boom is varnished spruce.

Originally, roller reefing was standard. All halyards are cleated at the mast(s) and mechanical advantage is achieved by means of old Merriman #2 winches. Located outboard of each cockpit coaming and on pedestals are Merriman #5 genoa winches. As is the case with the original roller reefing, this sail handling gear has outlived its usefulness and upgrades are well warranted. End-boom sheeting controls the main and is attached to a traveler located just forward of the hatch to the lazarette.

For auxiliary power, the Alberg 35 relies on the Universal Atomic Four. This venerable gasoline power plant is direct water-cooled and can provide a cruising speed of about 6 knots under calm conditions. The boat handles fine when steering forward; however, in reverse the boat backs poorly. This is due to the combination of a forward mounted rudder, a prop in an aperture, and a full keel. It takes practice and time to get used to it.

UNDER WAY

While the Alberg 35 was promoted as a racer/cruiser, it was and still is primarily a cruising sailboat. Its relatively narrow hull and heavy displacement make for an easy motion in a seaway and the ability to carry a modern cruiser's payload. Its displacement/waterline length ratio is 406.9, making it a very heavy displacement cruiser. Unlike more modern, wider beamed boats and despite its 42 percent ballast/displacement ratio, the Alberg 35 is a bit tender, and heels quickly. However, once it achieves 25-30 degrees, it stiffens up dramatically and, like most narrow boats, sails quite efficiently at fairly steep angles of heel.

*By the Numbers**

Ballast/Displacement Ratio 42%
Displacement/WaterlineLength Ratio 406.9
SailArea/DisplacementRatio. . .(sloop/yawl)16.1/17.23
CapsizeScreening Ratio 1.66
MotionComfort Ratio 34.59

*Refer to Appendix A for a complete discussion on how these ratios were obtained, what they mean, and how to use them.

THINGS TO CHECK OUT

Before you do anything, remember that the youngest Alberg 35 rolled off the line in 1967. For starters, check the decks for delamination caused by a balsa core saturated with water. Pay keen attention around fittings, such as cleats and stanchions. Delaminated areas sound dull and hollow when tapped with a plastic hammer or the handle of a screwdriver.

Mast compression is another potential problem. Look for signs of cracking, bending, or movement of the mast support beam and associated compression posts.

As with most sailboats of this vintage, the gelcoat may be crazed and faded. While this may be mainly a cosmetic problem, if too extensive, crazing can allow water to migrate into the laminate: then the problem becomes structural.

Don't forget to have the surveyor check for a possible void between the bottom ballast casting and the fiberglass shell. Inspect the wooden rudder for damage due to groundings and for corroded mounting bolts.

Since tankage can vary from boat to boat, take a closer look. It has been reported that early boats had galvanized tanks. These will eventually rust through.

As with any boat of this vintage, be prepared to address the wiring, sails and sail handling gear, the alcohol stove, electronics, and the Atomic Four.

OWNERS' COMMENTS

"...a solid, well-sailing boat...has a comfortable motion under way and is well-behaved under most circumstances..." Tom A., 1965 model

"...she sails well... have made two trips to Havana with grace and comfort...is sea-kindly...gets compliments for the graceful lines...if there is any negative, it's that she has a beam of 9'8"..." Greg C., 1961 model

"...boat performs well in heavy weather...handled 50-knot winds and 10-foot seas crossing the Gulf Stream and 35-knot winds and 12-foot following seas leaving Easter Island...this is a vessel you can feel safe and secure in..." Dorian L., 1967 model

SUMMING IT UP

While it may initially appear that the Alberg 35 is a tired, old, worn-out craft—not so. This boat was designed and built with reasonably heavy scantlings and is suitable for serious offshore sailing. Its classic lines are still appealing, causing heads to turn when the boat enters a marina. While it's the narrowest of this collection of twenty sailboats, its length compensates; a liveaboard couple will have plenty of room.

If you're looking to do some serious cruising, for the money, an Alberg 35 is hard to beat. It's true that repairs, modifications, and upgrades will add to price, but you won't break the bank or destroy your investment. Prices for an Alberg 35 range from $23,500 for a 1964 to $29,500 for a 1967 model.

"At sea, I learned how little a person needs, not how much."

Robin Lee Graham

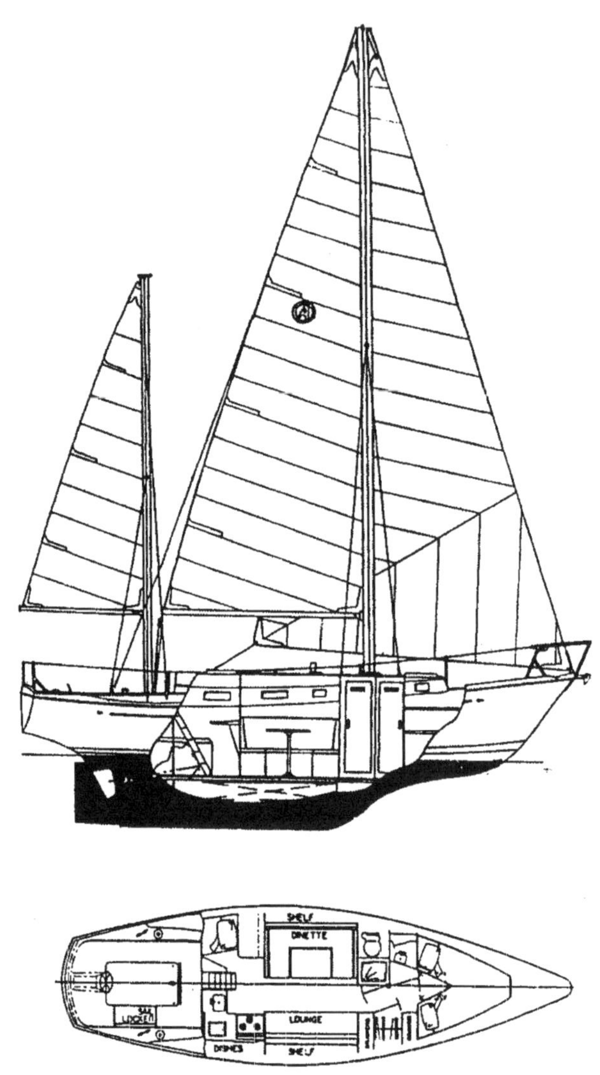

Allied Princess 36

Allied Princess 36

She will cross an ocean if you will.

The Allied Boat Company, Inc. officially went into business on February 9, 1962. Its offices and production facilities were established in a former brick plant located on Catskill Creek, just a stone's throw from the Hudson River and about 100 miles north of New York City. For the company's entire time in business (1962 through 1981), the Allied Boat Company remained at this location.

The company's first offering was the very successful, 30-foot, ketch-rigged Seawind 30. In marketing the Seawind 30, Allied's slogan was, "She'll cross an ocean if you will." In 1964, when the Seawind 30 became the first fiberglass boat to circumnavigate the world, these words became reality.

From the beginning, Allied capitalized on the talents of several notable naval architects to enhance its ever-expanding product line: these included Thomas Gillmer, Bill Luders, Britton Chance, and the firm of Sparkman and Stephens, to name a few.

Throughout much of its life, Allied was plagued with financial difficulties, suffered several changes in ownership, tolerated numerous personality conflicts, and endured escalating economic difficulties. This constant turmoil finally took its toll. In 1982, The Allied Boat Company closed its doors forever. Even with all of these "distractions," Allied was recognized as a high quality boatbuilder. And because of the plant's efficient production techniques, few boats were returned for rework. The Princess 36 is no exception.

DESIGN AND CONSTRUCTION

After graduating from the U.S. Coast Guard Academy and fulfilling his military commitment, naval architect Arthur H. Edmunds, Jr. began contributing designs to the Allied cruising boat product line. Among these was the Princess 36, a larger version of her little sister, the Seawind 30. Designed in May of 1972 and remaining in production until late 1981, the Princess 36 was probably Allied's most popular boat of the time. During its production run, approximately 140 Princess 36s were constructed.

The major design elements of the Princess 36 are a classic sheer, long counter, and a high bow. The design talents of Arthur H. Edmunds, Jr. produced a look that sets the Princess 36 apart from other boats.

The materials employed in fabricating the Princess 36 are those that were common to the 1970s; however, the techniques were slightly different. For the hull, the hand layup process incorporated the use of full hull-length layers of woven roving and mat, to which a final layer of cloth was added. This produced a very strong vessel. The thickness of the hull increases at the turn of the bilge and achieves its greatest thickness at the keel. The deck is a fiberglass laminate, with end-grain balsa being used as the coring material in all walking areas, cockpit sole, and cabin top. This type of deck construction increases the structural stiffness without adding any weight. On the negative side, balsa cored decks can suffer from compression, delamination, and rot if not properly maintained.

There is no interior pan or liner; all the bulkheads are bonded or tabbed to the hull and deck. This further enhances an already strong structure and substantiates Allied's reputation for building strong decks and hulls. To give the cabin overhead a finished look, the Princess 36 uses a one-piece headliner.

The hull-to-deck joint consists of an outside flange joint, commonly referred to as an outward flange. It is chemically bonded, mechanically fastened on 5-inch centers, glassed over, and finally covered with an aluminum extrusion. Unfortunately, outward-turning flanges are susceptible to damage from contact with docks and other things that a boat occasionally bumps into. It is the aluminum gunwale's primary function to hopefully protect this flange from such damage.

The keel cavity, an integral part of the hull mold, is filled with 5,000 pounds of lead ballast and then glassed over with two layers of mat and roving. This encapsulation process makes for a watertight bond. This is especially important should a puncture of the keel's fiberglass skin occur during a grounding.

The rudder of the Princess 36 is hung on the trailing edge of the keel and is controlled by Edson worm gear steering. The rudder post is 1½ inch bronze stock; it rides on a massive 32-pound bronze heel casting.

ON DECK

The high bow of the Princess 36, which gives the boat a significant amount of forward freeboard, is akin to a double-edged sword. While the look is striking, from a perception standpoint one experiences the definite sensation of walking uphill when going forward. As far as performance is concerned, the high bow hinders the boat's windward sailing ability, but at the same time keeps the boat drier in a seaway.

In addition to the mooring cleats and chocks on the foredeck, there's a pair of deck pipes leading below to a cavernous chain locker that is split into two sections.

On the cabin top, just forward of the mast, is an opening hatch. Abaft the mast is a pair of Dorade cowl vents. The cabin top exhibits a good deal of camber. This aids in water runoff and is quite distinctive. There are ten portlights—or, more correctly, deadlights, since none of them opens. Opening ports were optional and are an upgrade that would greatly improve the cabin's ventilation. Without them, there's only the forward hatch, the companionway, and a pair of cowl vents to direct airflow below.

Other on-deck features include a nonskid pattern molded into the gelcoat on all horizontal surfaces and a sea hood for the companionway's sliding hatch.

The cockpit is self-bailing and is a spacious 10 feet long and 6 feet wide. Because of the forward-facing wheel of the worm gear steering, it seems even larger. This is great for entertaining or sleeping under the stars, but not the best for offshore work. Fortunately, there's a bridge deck to help keep a flooded cockpit from spilling water below. Plus, the aft deck and steering housing aids in keeping the cockpit dry. While there's a mizzenmast to contend with, it's at the forward end of the cockpit and, on the plus side, does afford a solid handhold, especially for crew coming up from below. The coamings are reasonably high and provide good back support. Lastly, located beneath the starboard cockpit seat is a sail locker, which also allows additional access to the boat's mechanical systems.

BELOW DECK

The layout of the accommodations is very straightforward. There's a V-berth without a filler, whose port and starboard sides each measure a fairly generous 6 feet 7 inches by 2 feet 8 inches. Out and above are full-length fiddled shelves for stowing small items. For privacy, a solid teak door closes off the forward cabin from the rest of the boat. Abaft and to port is the head compartment, with the head separated from the sink and vanity by a half-bulkhead. In front of the head and close to the boat's centerline is the optional shower and sump. Privacy for the head compartment is afforded by another solid teak door. Opposite the head and to starboard is a relatively large hanging locker flanked on either side by a set of bureau drawers.

In the main saloon there's a U-shaped dinette arrangement to port and a single settee to starboard. Both settees measure 6 feet 6 inches in length; either makes for a decent sea berth. There's stowage behind and beneath the dinette and beneath the starboard settee, as well as a long fiddled shelf outboard and above, on the starboard side. While the U-shaped dinette was the standard configuration, the traditional arrangement of opposing settees with a bulkhead-mounted drop leaf table was an option. In either case, the main saloon is designed to be open and airy.

The L-shaped galley is to starboard and is comprised of an alcohol stove, a 7-cubic-foot icebox, and a centerline stainless steel sink with pressurized water. There are also manual pumps for seawater, icebox water, and potable water. The galley offers a good amount of stowage space for galleyware and dry goods. To port is a hinged-top chart table with a full suite of drawers beneath and a quarter berth aft.

Like the two main saloon berths, the quarter berth is 6 feet 6 inches long. Because of its proximity to the chart table, the quarter berth doubles as the chart table's seat.

All tankage is located beneath the cabin's sole. This includes the 80-gallon, stainless steel potable water tank and the 40-gallon fuel tank. Access to the engine and all its filters is gained by removing the companionway stairs and engine housing.

The Princess 36 exhibits an interior seemingly made entirely of wood. There's no fiberglass to be seen. Bulkheads, cabinets, and the like are plastic wood-grained laminates that have been trimmed with Burmese teak. The sole and all accessory pieces, such as handrails and stairs, are also teak. Even with a generous 6 feet 4 inches of headroom, the darkness of the finish courts claustrophobia. Many owners have resorted to painting the laminate white and varnishing the teak trim.

SPECIFICATIONS

LOA	36'0"
LWL	27'6"
Beam	11'0"
Draft	4'6"
Displacement	14,400 lbs.
Ballast	5,000 lbs.
Sail Area	(sloop/ketch) 595/604 sq. ft.

THE RIG

The original Princess 36 was available as either a ketch or a sloop, with the ketch being the most popular. The sail area/displacement ratio is 16.3 for the ketch and 16.1 for the sloop. In late 1977, the Princess II was introduced. Since she came with a bowsprit, this boat was able to offer a cutter rig option. Even though the Princess II came with an enclosed quarter cabin, a deeper draft (5 feet 1 inch), and larger cockpit drains, the differences between the two models were not significant enough to greatly influence a buying decision. Of the more than 140 Princesses built, only a dozen are Princess IIs.

Both masts, main and mizzen, are stepped on deck and each employs a single pair of spreaders. All spars are anodized aluminum extrusions with internal sail tracks. The shrouds are outboard and secured to chain plates that have most of their length buried in fiberglass gussets. One important standard feature of the Princess 36 is that all standing rigging is comprised of oversized stainless steel wire with swagged terminals.

The main mast towers 46 feet above the waterline. All halyards are cleated at the masts, there is end-boom sheeting for both main and mizzen, and the Barlow headsail sheet winches are located on the cockpit coamings.

The Princess 36 came standard with a 25 hp Westerbeke diesel engine with a 2:1 reduction gear. The power plant is freshwater-cooled and turns a 17x11 three-blade propeller. This combination provides decent thrust as well as noticeable drag when under sail. Handling in reverse elicits the usual complaints.

UNDER WAY

The Princess 36 tracks well and, because of her multiple sail rig, can be balanced nicely—that is, assuming that the proper combination of sails is set. Douse the main and sail with a "jib 'n jigger" whenever the wind pipes up. When anchored, leave the mizzen up to help steady the boat. Don't forget to douse the mizzen when reaching. On this point of sail, it has a tendency to increase weather helm.

The boat's high forward freeboard negatively affects its windward sailing ability. Performance (speed), both upwind and off the wind, can be rated as average.

With a displacement/waterline length ratio of 309.1, the Princess 36 is considered a heavy displacement cruiser. However, some feel that the boat is initially tender (a relative term), but stiffens up nicely. She will rarely bury her rail.

The worm gear steering is super, and boats fitted with steering vanes perform very well. This is a cruising sailboat, not an offshore racer.

BY THE NUMBERS

Ballast/Displacement Ratio 35%
Displacement/WaterlineLength Ratio 309.11
Sail Area/Displacement Ratio (ketch/sloop)16.33/16.08
Capsize Screening Ratio 1.81
Motion Comfort Ratio 30.16

THINGS TO CHECK OUT

Besides the usual deck delamination/compression, tired power plant, and outdated system components, there are several areas specific to the Princess 36 to which one needs to pay particular attention:

Inspect the chain plates. Crevice corrosion has been responsible for failures and can lead to a dismasting.

The Princess 36 has a large cockpit, but unfortunately the cockpit drains aren't correspondingly large enough. However, those of the Princess II are oversized and drain the cockpit nicely.

Check out the bulkhead tabbing. Because of continual flexing, breaks can and do occur. Fortunately, the fix is not difficult. Also investigate the outward deck-to-hull joint for possible damage and water seepage.

While most boats were fitted with worm gear steering, a few came off the line with either rack and pinion or chain-driven pull-pull systems.

Tankage is another area that needs to be looked into. Fuel tank volumes vary from 37 to 70 gallons. Tanks were either black iron or steel; steel makes the better tank. Also, potable water volumes can range from 60-100 gallons.

OWNER'S COMMENTS

"...over the years I've fixed just about everything: deck rot, rusted fuel tank, new chain plates, and even painted her from top to bottom...wouldn't trade her or my wife for a newer model..." Stan L., 1977 model

SUMMING IT UP

The Princess 36 may not be a fast boat, but she is a comfortable, seaworthy cruising boat. The Allied Boat Company had a reputation for building strong boats, and the Princess 36 is no exception. True, her shoal draft contributes to her initial tenderness, and the large cockpit is not the best for offshore work. However, many a Princess 36 has visited a foreign port and several have circumnavigated the world. The ketch rig and cruising layout are versatile and will satisfy casual sailor and serious cruiser alike.

Her robust construction, bulletproof rigging, worm gear steering, and good sea berths are a plus. Add to this her economy—a Princess 36 ranges from $30,000 to $60,000; a Princess II is about $7,000 higher—and you have a real value.

"There is a compelling simplicity about making headway under sail;
no moving parts, no lubrication or fuel, no noise—
just the wind in the sails and the boat in harmony with nature."

John Beattie, *The Breath of Angels*, 1997

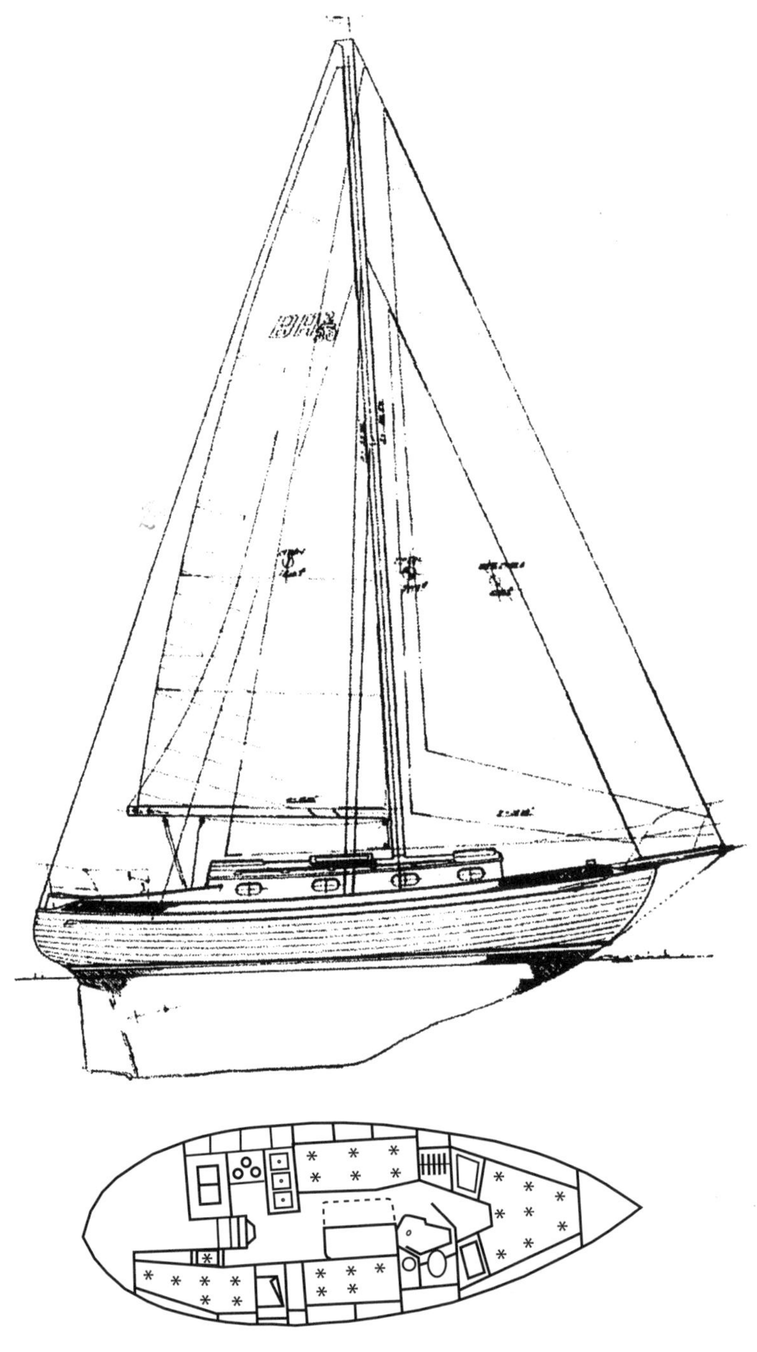

Baba 30

BABA 30

A roomy, traditional, double-ender.

A Seattle, Washington yacht broker by the name of Robert Berg had a vision of a traditionally styled cruising yacht that would be both faster and less expensive than the then-popular Westsail 32. In the mid 1970s, this vision became a reality when he, along with two business associates, formed Flying Dutchman International Ltd. While Flying Dutchman was not a boat building enterprise, the company's charter was to design boats, have them built in the Far East to their specifications, and then import them.

Ta Shing Boatbuilders, whose reputation was the best in Taiwan and among the best in the world, was selected as Flying Dutchman's boat manufacturer. As the designer, Berg commissioned noted naval architect Bob Perry. This was not a casual selection on the part of Berg. For his boat, Berg envisioned a smaller version of the Tayana 37, one of Perry's most popular designs.

With the corporation set up, the manufacturer selected, and the designer commissioned, Robert Berg went about personally designing the boat's interior. Keeping in mind long-distance cruising, Berg offered two interior configurations: a V-berth model (that would become popular on the West Coast), and a double berth model (that would be favored by East Coast sailors).

All that remained was to find a name. The Taiwanese took care of that. The name Baba originated from the local Chinese slang version of Bob Berg's name.

Production of the Baba 30 began in 1977, with the first model entering the marketplace in 1978. Two hundred and thirty Baba 30s were produced during its eight-year production run, which ceased in 1985 with the demise of Flying Dutchman International. It's been over twenty years since the last Baba 30 was built, yet it remains a favorite of cruising couples.

Design and Construction

Bob Perry drew the Baba 30 to be a relatively heavy, rather beamy, traditional, double-ended, blue-water cruiser. Its hand-laminated, uncored, fiberglass reinforced plastic (FRP) hull was designed to meet or exceed Lloyds specifications. In fact, a Lloyds certificate was originally available at an additional cost.

Fabrication of the hull was achieved by using alternating layers of fiberglass mat and woven roving. In most places there are approximately six layers. Hull thickness is increased at the keel area, where there are close to a dozen layers. The topsides exhibit considerable flair, which enhances stability and also keeps the boat dry when working to weather.

The deck is also hand laminated FRP; however, all horizontal surfaces are cored with end-grain balsa. This sandwiching is strong yet lightweight. The hull-to-deck joint is chemically bonded, mechanically fastened with stainless steel bolts, and cosmetically finished with a teak caprail.

The boat has a full keel with a cutaway forefoot. This design enhances the boat's maneuverability without detracting from her tracking ability. The 4,000 pounds of ballast is internal and is comprised of a single cast iron ingot. For structural integrity, the keel cavity is glassed over.

The rudder has a straight aft edge and its bottom angles slightly upward going aft. It's mounted on the trailing edge of the keel, with the rudder post appearing well aft in the cockpit. This frees valuable space in an already small cockpit, especially if a tiller is employed.

ON DECK

One of the most notable deck features is the laminated FRP bowsprit. It measures 4 feet in length, is surrounded by a stainless steel bow pulpit, and is the home of the dual integrated anchor rollers as well as a bronze windlass. Slightly aft of this promontory is a pair of deck pipes that lead to a large chain locker. Completing the anchoring/mooring hardware is a Sampson post and six hawse holes and horn cleats (two forward, two amidships, and two stern). All deck hardware has been through-bolted and backed with stainless steel mounting plates.

Many boats were delivered with textured, nonskid surfaces on the deck and cabin tops, while others were overlaid with teak. The deck perimeter is defined by a low bulwark/high toe rail that measures 3 inches in height and encloses 18-inch-wide sidedecks.

There is an opening teak hatch located at the forward end of the cabin top, as well as a large, teak butterfly hatch/skylight situated amidships, over the main saloon. Eight bronze opening portlights and a pair of Dorade cowl vents provide additional illumination and ventilation. Entrance through the companionway is by means a pair of louvered teak doors (for style) as well as a series of hatch boards (for function). Add to this a sea hood and the package is complete.

The cockpit, at approximately 60 inches long, is a bit smallish but workable. Two 2-inch scuppers make it self-bailing, and the bridge deck contains any water from cascading down below. The entire seating area is teak overlay. Cockpit stowage includes a large seat locker to port, a pair of port and starboard cubbies with doors located high in the coamings, a vented locker in which to secure a single 5-gallon propane bottle, and two oval-shaped compartments in the aft backrests. While tiller steering frees up valuable space in the relatively small cockpit, pedestal-mounted wheel steering is very common.

Below Deck

The efficient, compact layout is designed for two adults to cruise in comfort, though it can accommodate additional passengers. Two Bob Berg designs were built, offering a choice of sleeping accommodations for four or five. One design included a large double berth forward with lockers and drawers below, plus louvered lockers and shelves port and starboard. The second design was built with a traditional V-berth with filler, lockers below, and louvered lockers and shelves port and starboard. Access to the forepeak/chain locker is through teak louvered doors. Speaking of doors, when swung all the way open, the head compartment door gives privacy to the forward compartment.

Abaft and to port is a hanging locker with a louvered door, and on the starboard side is the head compartment. The head's interior bulkheads and countertops are a plastic laminate. This enclosed compartment is functional, albeit a bit small. It houses a circular stainless steel sink with pressurized hot and cold water, a mirror, louvered locker, shower, and, of course, the centerline-facing head.

The main saloon's spaciousness is partly attributable to the boat's 10-foot 6-inch beam and its 6-foot 4-inch headroom. Its arrangement is quite typical, with port and starboard settees and either a bulkhead-mounted or a fixed-pedestal drop leaf table. The port settee is 6 feet long, while the starboard one measures only 4 feet 2 inches. Stowage abounds, with several large and deep compartments, lockers, and shelves. The tankage, both water and fuel, is situated beneath the settees. Volumes range from 25 to 40 gallons for fuel and 40 to 80 gallons for potable water.

The portside galley is U-shaped and is an extremely efficient arrangement. It has a well-insulated top-loading icebox, a large asbestos/stainless steel lined stove area that can easily accommodate a gimbaled 3-burner stove/oven, and dual stainless steel sinks with manual fresh and seawater pumps as well as pressurized hot and cold water. There are numerous drawers, dry lockers, and shelves throughout the galley area.

To starboard is the forward-facing navigation station with hinged chart table stowage and a locker beneath, generous shelving outboard and above, and adequate surface mounting space for instrumentation and communications gear. Abaft is the 68-inch by 30-inch quarter berth with stowage beneath. Tucked between this berth and the companionway stairs is a convenient wet locker.

Engine access, which is average, is obtained by removing the companionway stairs and engine compartment housing.

Galley counter surfaces are a plastic laminate, while—depending upon the year—the exposed interior hulls are either smooth gelcoat that's been covered with a quilted vinyl, or an insulating and sound-deadening sprayed-on foam battened with teak. All other interior surfaces are teak. The cabinetry and joinery are of high quality. The sole is teak and holly and overhead are teak grabrails.

Specifications

LOA	34'6"
LOD	29'9"
LWL	24'6"
Beam	10'3"
Draft	4'9"
Displacement	12,500 lbs.
Ballast	4,000 lbs.
Sail Area	504 sq. ft.

The Rig

The Baba 30 has a tall cutter rig whose sail area/displacement ratio is 14.97. Its mast is stepped on deck and is supported by a single pair of cap shrouds, fore and aft lowers, a single pair of spreaders, a backstay, and a headstay. Depending upon the year of production, the spars can either be spruce or anodized aluminum. The combination of a jib, staysail, and main yields a sail area of 504 square feet. The main came standard with two reef points and jiffy reefing. Most earlier boats were equipped with self-tending staysails, while later models incorporated a boom gallows. Located on the cabin top are the staysail's sheet tracks and outboard on the side decks are the jib's sheet tracks. The main sheet attaches to a traveler situated on either the bridge deck or on an arch that spans the forward portion of the companionway hatch. The number and manufacturer of winches varies, with seven Barients being the most common (three on the mast, two on the coamings, and two on the cabin top).

Engine manufacturers also vary. A 23 hp Volvo diesel was original equipment. However, Perkins and Yanmar diesels also found their way aboard.

Under Way

Even though the Baba 30 sports a tall cutter rig, its somewhat low sail area/displacement ratio of 14.97 combined with its displacement/waterline length ratio of 379 makes for lackluster light air performance. Here's where a big genoa can really help out. In light wind, a main and genoa perform quite well, especially when reaching or on a run.

As the wind begins to pipe up, so does the boat's performance. The following general set of rules may help set up the boat, but are dependent upon sail trim and the state of the sea:

The boat's full complement of sails performs well up to about 15 knots. At about 15-18 knots, a single reef in the main balances the boat nicely and allows it to sail on its feet. This is assuming that both headsails are up. As the wind increases to 15-25 knots, the working jib and shortened main should be sufficient. At 20-30 knots, swap the working jib for the staysail. Take a second tuck in the main at around 30-35 knots, and beyond 35 knots, it's trysail and storm jib or possibly staysail.

Regardless of which engine the boat is equipped with, its rating is adequate for acceptable forward progress. However, like all boats with a full keel, backing up under power can be challenging.

The Baba 30's low capsize screening ratio and relatively high motion comfort ratio makes for a sea-kindly ride in all types of sea conditions. The resultant slower motion makes for more comfort and a steadier working platform.

By the Numbers

Ballast/Displacement Ratio	32%
Displacement/Waterline Length Ratio	379.46
Sail Area/Displacement Ratio	14.97
Capsize Screening Ratio	1.77
Motion Comfort Ratio	13.15

Things to Check Out

Check the decks and cabin top for signs of delamination caused by a balsa core that has been saturated with water. End-grain balsa is good at limiting the spread of moisture, but a wet core, no matter how small the area, is a problem. Pay keen attention around all fittings. The fasteners on teak decks are notorious for contributing to core delamination. With the mast being stepped on deck, look for possible mast compression of the balsa core.

A few of the earlier boats came with only a single set of shrouds. This is definitely an area that will need to be upgraded. There have been reports of corroded chain plate bolts. These are easily inspected from below and should be routinely monitored.

Some minor osmotic blistering has been noted near the waterline. While this is somewhat cosmetic in nature, if it is not addressed properly, additional water penetration and further damage is likely to occur.

If the boat is equipped with a steel fuel tank, it should be inspected carefully for signs of corrosion, both in and out.

Lastly, the Baba 30 is festooned with brightwork, both in and out. Care or neglect over the years will be readily apparent. In any case, this will be an ongoing maintenance issue.

OWNER'S COMMENTS

"...amazing the load she'll carry...largest and safest 30-footer out there cruising...sailed from Hawaii to Fiji and back and averaged 100 miles a day (we sail conservative)..." Carl P., 1977 model

SUMMING IT UP

The Baba 30 is an affordable blue-water cruiser with a very accommodating interior, seaworthy sailing capabilities, and the classic cruising yacht look. In light winds, she's an underperformer; however, when the wind freshens, her performance increases. With her broad beam, standing headroom, and numerous stowage compartments, the Baba 30 can easily carry a couple and all their cruising stores to many a far-off land. Once there, her owners can spend many a leisure hour maintaining the boat's brightwork. Baba 30s range in price from $50,000 for a 1978 model to near $70,000 for a 1984 version.

"One of the benefits of depending almost exclusively on sails is that you'll have the joy of working into the same anchorages that Columbus, Drake, Cook, and Nelson entered under sail alone."

Lin and Larry Pardey

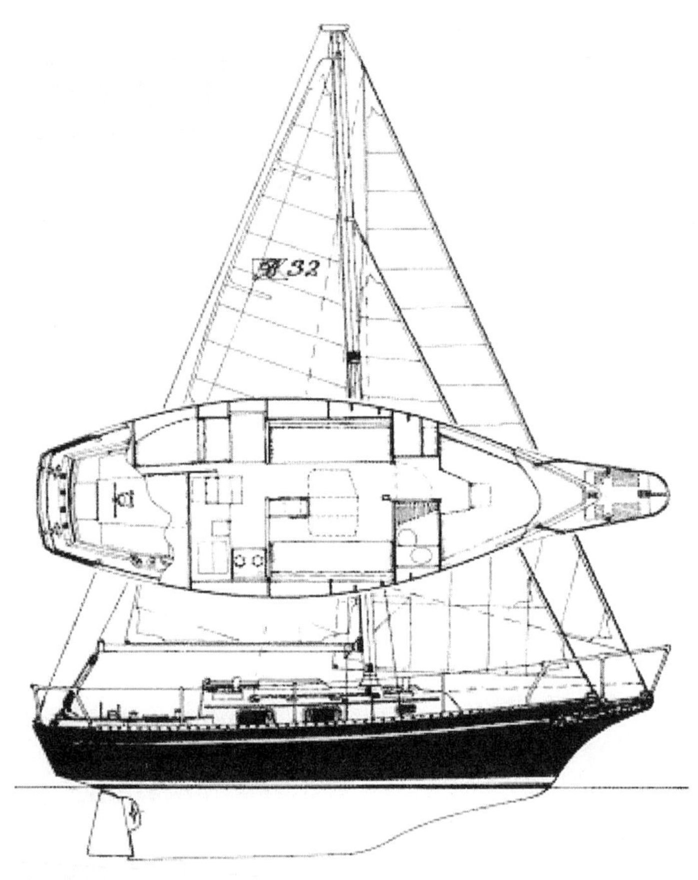

Bayfield 32

Bayfield 32

Traditionally modern.

In the early 1970s, Bayfield Boat Yard Limited of Bayfield, Ontario embarked upon creating a family of full-keeled, clipper-bowed cruising boats. At the design helm was naval architect Hedley "Ted" Gozzard. With the exception of the Bayfield 36—which was designed by Ted's younger brother, Hayden—all of the line came from Ted's drafting board.

The first boat to be introduced was thc Bayfield 25. In contrast to its fin-keeled, racer/cruiser contemporaries, the Bayfield 25 had standing headroom and an inboard diesel, and drew less than three feet of water. The concept was well received, and in 1973 the Bayfield 32 made its appearance. The boat was originally known as the Bayfield 30, owing to the fact that it was really a 30-foot boat. However, U.S. dealers insisted on calling it a 32, measuring the LOA to include the clipper bow and trail boards. Reason gave way to marketing and the rest is history. The boat was a huge success; about 300 additional 32s were built before production ceased in 1990.

Over the years, the company tinkered with the boat in many ways, though its basic dimensions and design stayed the same. The boat sported at least three different mast heights; at one point, the company even made a couple of ketches. Engine installations ranged from a Sperry-Vickers hydraulic drive, to Mercedes diesels, and finally to single- and twin-cylinder Yanmars. The number and style of ports varied, and the hardware was modified as time went on. Most Bayfield 32s were festooned with teak; however, two boats were outfitted with black walnut interiors.

In July of 1981, H. Ted Gozzard sold his interest in Bayfield Boat Works and shortly thereafter, in February 1982, founded North Castle Marine Ltd./Gozzard Yachts. After Ted left the company, Bayfield Boat Works underwent changes in management and partnerships. The company continued to build boats until it ceased operations around the turn of the decade.

The Bayfield 32 is a pure cruising boat with a salty personality, as evidenced by its clipper bow with trail boards and mahogany taffrail supported by turned spindles. Many have crisscrossed the Caribbean, while a few have made ocean crossings.

DESIGN AND CONSTRUCTION

The Bayfield 32's design is characterized by a somewhat exaggerated clipper bow, complete with carved wooden trail boards, a noticeably raked transom, and a handsome traditional sheer. The underwater profile is that of a full keel with a moderate cutaway forefoot of rather shallow draft. Completing the package is a low aspect ratio masthead cutter rig and a maximum beam that occurs amidships.

The basic construction of the boat is straightforward, with a few subtle nuances. The hull and overhead liner are comprised of handlaid alternating layers of fiberglass mat and woven roving. Three-eighths-inch balsa is used as the coring material in both the deck and hull liner. This construction technique adds strength and structure without adding additional weight. The balsa coring also contributes significant sound and temperature insulation. For additional strength, the sea hood, sliding companionway hatch, and cockpit hatch covers are cored with plywood.

The hull-to-deck joint is chemically bonded and is mechanically fastened every six inches with stainless steel bolts. These bolts are also used to secure the extruded aluminum toe rail to the top of the low fiberglass bulwarks.

ON DECK

Except for the stemhead fitting, the mooring cleats, and the staysail tack fitting, the boat's foredeck is clutter-free. Add to this a nonskid textured surface and a teak-covered clipper bow surrounded by a stainless steel bow pulpit, and one has a fairly secure area to move freely about. The side decks, which are reasonably wide, are bordered by short bulwarks capped with a slotted aluminum toe rail.

Forward on the cabin is a translucent hatch accompanied by a Dorade ventilator to starboard. A second Dorade ventilator is located farther aft on the starboard side. The companionway is situated off-center and slightly to port. Its sliding hatch incorporates a sea hood. Teak handrails are mounted on either side of the cabin top.

The cockpit is self-bailing and offers high, sloped coamings that provide very good back support and a feeling of being "down and in." The coamings are capped with teak, while the stern features a taffrail with turned spindles followed farther aft by a stainless steel stern pulpit. There's a pair of generous cockpit lockers situated port and starboard, a couple of coaming cubbies, and a vented propane locker beneath the helmsman seat. The propane locker can house a pair of 10-pound tanks. Wheel steering is standard.

BELOW DECK

The Bayfield 32 combines a molded fiberglass overhead liner and a pan or hull liner, not only to add structural integrity, but also to designate the location of interior features. While gelcoated liners are often seen as the finished interior surface on many boats, this is not the case with the Bayfield 32. Teak, both solid and veneer, is extensively used throughout the boat, including a teak shower grating, ice grate in the icebox, and, of course, a teak and holly sole. This use of natural wood gives the cabin a warm, traditional appearance.

The amount of interior space is quite surprising, and the accommodations are straightforward. The forward compartment consists of a generous V-berth with filler, followed to starboard by the head, with stainless steel sink, shower, and pressurized cold water. To port is a hanging locker and a series of drawers. Additional stowage can be found in drawers beneath the V-berth and on port and starboard fiddled shelves located above and outboard. Ventilation and illumination for the V-berth are achieved by means of the forward hatch. The head has an opening portlight and a Dorade ventilator. The door to the head performs a dual role. It will isolate and give privacy to the head or to the entire forward section.

Abaft the forward compartment bulkhead is the main cabin with its opposing settees and a drop leaf table to starboard. While most Bayfield 32s feature a bulkhead-mounted table with shelving behind, earlier models featured an L-shaped dinette with a fixed pedestal table. In either case the starboard settee converts to a double berth, giving the main cabin berths for three.

There is a partial bulkhead aft and to starboard, which defines the beginning of the galley area. The galley includes an alcohol stove with oven, a 4-cubic-foot icebox, and a single stainless steel sink with pressurized cold water and manual sea water. There's sufficient stowage for galleyware and dry goods and adequate counter space, if one includes the companionway step area. Ventilation for the galley is by means of a Dorade ventilator. Potable water tankage has been reported from 20-40 gallons, with 20 gallons being the acceptable norm.

Across from the galley, on the port side, is the forward-facing navigation station. The quarter berth, situated just aft of the chart table, functions both as a good sea berth and as the seat for the chart table.

There are teak grab rails on either side of the cabin overhead for good bracing in a seaway, as well as 6-plus feet of headroom for ease of movement.

Over the years, the total number of portlights as well as the number of fixed and opening ones has varied. Originally, the boat was equipped with five fixed and one opening in the head area. In later years, the total number of six portlights was increased to eight. Also standard is a forward translucent hatch and a pair of Dorade ventilators, forward and aft on the starboard side.

As any sailor knows, stowage on a sailboat is a precious commodity. The Bayfield 32 has abundant stowage—under and behind settees/berths, beneath the quarter berth, in or behind the table in the main saloon—as well as good cockpit locker space.

SPECIFICATIONS

LOA	32'0"
LWL	23'3"
Beam	10'6"
Draft	3'9"
Displacement	9,600 lbs.
Ballast	4,000 lbs.
Sail Area	525 sq. ft.

THE RIG

The standard Bayfield 32 has a bridge clearance of 45 feet from its DWL to the top of its keel-stepped mast. There is also a "C" version of the Bayfield 32. It has a mast 4 feet taller and has an additional 3 feet of bowsprit compared to the standard yacht. This increases the sail area from 525 square feet to 662 square feet. The sail/displacement ratio of the standard version is 18.6. It is a masthead cutter rig with a low aspect ratio. Standing rigging includes a pair of cap shrouds, fore and aft lower shrouds, a backstay, and topping lift. The spars are anodized aluminum extrusions with internal sail tracks. The staysail tracks are located inboard on the side decks, while the genoa tracks are situated on the bulwarks. For control of the headsails' sheets, there are two primary two-speed and two secondary single-speed winches mounted on the cockpit coamings. The main sheet extends from the end of the boom and is cleated on a traveler situated on the transom. Completing the controls are three halyard winches and associated cleats mounted on the aft coach roof, two to starboard and one to port. With this, all control lines are led aft.

For auxiliary power, most Bayfield 32s rely on a 15 hp, freshwater cooled Yanmar diesel. However, there have been reports of 21 and 24 hp units also in use. Regardless of the engine's size, the boat's full keel makes backing under power adventurous. Fuel capacity has been reported anywhere from 12 to 25 gallons, with 20 gallons being the norm. Engine access is rated as good.

UNDER WAY

The boat is a cruiser, not a racer/cruiser. Because of its shoal draft, full keel, the boat will certainly not point to weather as compared to a deeper fin keel yacht. However, the keel's area is large enough to keep leeway moderate. With a displacement/waterline length ratio of 330.2, the Bayfield 32 is solid under foot and has a nice motion. The boat has good directional stability and the shoal keel allows for thin water exploration. In a freshening wind (15+ knots) 6 knots is easily achieved. While the dual headsails divide up the sail area and add versatility, the large mainsail makes the boat easy to handle under mainsail alone. Even though a respectable 5 knots or so can be achieved with a breeze of 10-12 knots, the boat's light air performance suffers. The "C" mode, with its higher mast and longer bowsprit, was introduced to minimize this deficiency.

BY THE NUMBERS

Ballast/Displacement Ratio	42%
Displacement/Waterline Length Ratio	330.23
Sail Area/Displacement Ratio	18.6
Capsize Screening Ratio	1.98
Motion Comfort Ratio	24.68

THINGS TO CHECK OUT

As with all boats that have cored balsa decks, sound out the Bayfield to determine if water intrusion and possibly delamination has taken place. Pay particular attention to areas under and around deck fittings, especially stanchions.

Investigate the wood support beneath the bowsprit. There have been reports of failures due to rot. While in that area, examine the trail boards. Many have been stripped off by large waves. Their lower edge extends below the fiberglass bow; when water is forced between and behind, the boards can separate from the boat.

Lastly, several Bayfield 32s that have been exposed to saltwater have reported corrosion and subsequent fuel tank failures.

OWNER'S COMMENTS

"...The full keel is wonderful except in harbor where it is a bit of a dog to swing around...good for a couple cruising...Great looking boat, just be ready for a little elbow grease with the exterior teak...overall a lot of boat for not a lot of money..."

Mark T., 1981 model

SUMMING IT UP

There's no mistaking the Bayfield 32 for anything but a cruiser. Its design and appearance is classic, its interior spacious and comfortable.

Windward performance is not a strong point of this boat. Keep it moving at a generous angle to the wind and you'll get to where you want to go. Light air will be challenging and maybe even a bit frustrating, but in heavy air with a double-reefed main and staysail, she'll do 6 knots, with no fuss and no water coming on board.

Prices for a Bayfield 32 range from under $20,000 for a 1977 model to $55,000 for a 1989 vintage boat.

"A little theory goes a long way towards developing
an understanding of how a sailboat works,
but getting in the boat and actually sailing is more fun."

John Rousemaniere

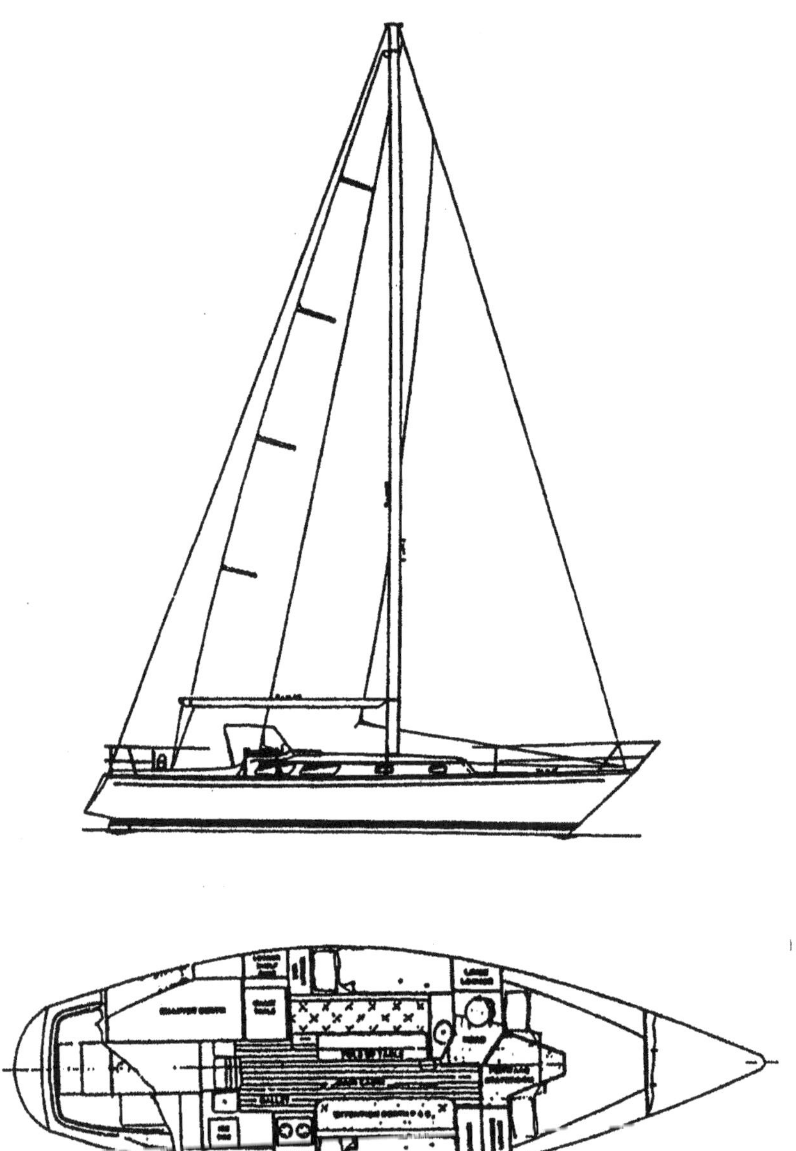

BRISTOL 35.5

Bristol 35.5

A semi-custom performance cruiser with staying power.

Six years after Clint and Everett Pearson sold Pearson Yachts to Grumman Industries, Clint Pearson formed Bristol Yachts. The year was 1966. In the eleven years that followed, Bristol Yachts built a number of traditionally styled boats that were designed by several leading traditional designers including Carl Alberg, John Alden, and Halsey Herreshoff. In 1977, consumers became interested in greater accommodations and more modern styling. Responding to market pressures, Clint enlisted the talents of Ted Hood. The result was the Bristol 35.5, a responsive yet comfortable performance cruiser.

The Bristol 35.5 was available in both a full keel version and a keel/centerboarder, the Bristol 35.5C. While the fixed keel version draws 5 feet 9 inches and the centerboard version 3 feet 9 inches to 9 feet 6 inches, both are of medium displacement, exhibiting a displacement/waterline length ratio of 321.9.

The boat was a subtle yet far-reaching departure from the rather ordinary boats the company had been producing up until that time. The Bristol 35.5 met the market challenges head on, and at the same time successfully showcased the quality of workmanship and structural integrity that was to become the hallmark of Bristol Yachts. With the success of the Bristol 35.5, most of Bristol's subsequent boats would come from the drafting table of Ted Hood. The Bristol 35.5 stood the test of time and remained in production until the company folded in 1997.

DESIGN AND CONSTRUCTION

In actuality, the Bristol 35.5 is quite orthodox. There are no real extremes in design or in construction. If anything, the design is on the conservative side and the construction tends to be a bit heavy. However, the boat's roomy accommodations, surprising performance, and quality of materials and workmanship really set it apart from other semicustom offerings.

The hull of the Bristol 35.5 is comprised of polyester resin and alternating layers of fiberglass, using mostly woven roving and, to a lesser proportion, fiberglass mat. The solid fiberglass hull is handlaid and is built in two halves and joined down the centerline. A three-inch inward-facing flange is integrally molded slightly below the top edge of the hull to receive the deck. The resulting hull-to-deck joint is then bonded with adhesive and through-bolted. A teak toe rail is also through-bolted and used to cap the joint. This adds significant rigidity. The deck is a fiberglass composite, handlaid with mat and cloth, and cored with end-grain balsa. Deck and hull thickness vary to suit structural demands.

While there is a fiberglass headliner in the Bristol 35.5, Bristol Yachts never extensively used fiberglass hull liners or pans as a structural component. They relied on traditional techniques that used wood as the structural member. All bulkheads, as well as athwartship and longitudinal members, are bonded to the hull with fiberglass and resin.

The rudder is fiberglass that is molded around bronze plates welded to a bronze rudder post. It's mounted to a skeg and rides on a bearing and a bronze rudder shoe.

The centerboard of the C model is also of fiberglass construction, but with internal lead ballast. A stainless steel wire rope runs along bronze sheaves and through a stainless steel pipe to a centerboard winch located on the aft of the cabin house.

Ballast is encapsulated lead: 6,500 pounds for the fin keel and 7,000 pounds for the centerboarder. The additional 500 pounds of ballast of the C model is contained in the centerboard, hence the need for a centerboard winch.

ON DECK

The deck of the Bristol 35.5 reflects careful planning. The deck, cabin top, cockpit seats, and cockpit sole feature a nonskid pattern. The foredeck, luxuriously spacious, is a first-rate work platform. The forward cabin-top hatch is large enough to permit the passing of sailbags. There's a pair of Dorade ventilators just forward of the mast and a second hatch over the main saloon. The molded sea hood is standard, and the molded-in ridge that extends from the sea hood aft is a perfect mount for a dodger. There are eight portlights. The four forward are opening, while the later four are fixed and considerably larger. The side decks are wide; the shrouds are outboard.

The spacious cockpit features two full-length seats. Surprisingly, there is no bridge deck to protect the cabin from water cascading below because of a pooped cockpit. When offshore, it would be prudent to keep the lower hatchboard securely in place.

The large wheel and the unique binnacle guard make for interesting gymnastics when trying to change helmsmen. A smaller wheel could help solve the problem. The coamings are reasonably high and offer decent back support. Stowage can be found in port and starboard seat lockers, the lazarette, and for small items, in the pair of coaming cubbies. All trim—including the toe rail, handrails, coach roof "eyebrows," and coaming caps—is teak.

BELOW DECK

Like the deck above, below deck the layout provides for a comfortable, uncramped, and uncluttered feeling. It is easy to move about, especially with the generous 6 feet 2 inches of headroom. Over the years, few changes to the accommodations have been made. Early on, there were three different layouts, including a choice of one, two, or no pilot berths in the main saloon. Fortunately, most boats came configured without pilot berths, thus making the amount of storage space excellent for cruising. Another variation was the configuration of the galley, either L- or U-shaped. Either one works well.

In the forward cabin there is a very adequate V-berth with filler piece. Stowage can be found beneath the berth and above, and outboard in lockers with caned inserts. There are four lockers total, two to port and two to starboard. The chain locker can also be accessed from the forward cabin. Immediately aft and to starboard are a hanging locker, a suite of drawers, and a shelf. There's a privacy door for the forward cabin and en suite entrance to the head. Ventilation and illumination are by means of the overhead forward hatch and a pair of opening portlights.

The head is located to port and, in addition to the forward cabin's privacy door, has a second entrance from the main saloon. There's a single stainless steel sink with pressurized hot and cold water and a handheld showerhead. There's also a vanity with stowage beneath and a linen locker outboard. A teak floor grate covers the molded fiberglass sole. There's an opening portlight and a Dorade ventilator.

The main saloon is amidships and features the traditional centerline-facing settees. Both have pullout extensions that form double berths. Lockers and fiddled shelves are situated over both port and starboard settees. To port is a bulkhead-mounted drop leaf table. A Dorade ventilator, a pair of opening portlights, and an overhead hatch provide ventilation and light. Four fixed portlights give additional illumination.

The relatively spacious and efficient galley is located to starboard and adjacent to the companionway for good ventilation. Its location also helps to keep the cook in close contact with the cockpit. The area combines a large counter surface and ample dry-goods stowage, with a deep, single stainless steel sink (pressurized hot and cold water); a large, well-insulated icebox; and a three-burner alcohol stove with oven.

The forward-facing navigation area is located to port. It shares the seat of the quarter berth directly aft. There's a full-sized chart table with ample room for chart storage under the lift-top table. The outboard shelves and locker can easily accommodate books and electronic equipment.

Many interiors are teak, but mahogany (Brunzeel bulkheads and Honduras trim), and American cherry are also available. The cabin sole is solid teak with ash inlay, all handlaid, screwed, glued, bunged, and sealed. Regardless of the choice of wood, the joinery reflects the high degree of skill exhibited by the craftsmen at Bristol Yachts.

Engine access for such routine maintenance as changing the oil filter or adjusting the packing gland is mediocre at best. Access to the narrow compartment is accomplished, in front, by removing several drawers and the awkward companionway stair panel. A panel in the quarter berth affords access on the port side.

The aluminum fuel tank, which holds approximately 31 gallons, is located on the centerline, aft of the engine and beneath the cockpit sole. Two stainless steel potable water tanks, one in the bow and a second beneath the cabin sole, hold the combined volume of 100 gallons.

SPECIFICATIONS

LOA	35'6"
LWL	27'6"
Beam	10'10"
Draft	(keel/cb) 5'9" /3'9"-9'6"
Displacement	15,000 lbs.
Ballast	(keel/cb) 6,500 lbs./7,000 lbs.
Sail Area	589 sq. ft.

THE RIG

The Bristol 35.5 is a keel-stepped, masthead-rigged sloop having a sail area of 589 square feet, comprised of a Bermudan main and 120 percent jib. Its sail area/displacement ratio is a moderate 15.5. The rig incorporates a pair of tapered spreaders with the standing rigging consisting of a head stay, a single pair of cap shrouds, fore and aft lower, and a backstay, all of which are 5/16 inch 7 x19 stainless steel wire rope. Both spars are anodized aluminum extrusions with stainless steel fittings. The jib tracks are 1¼-inch aluminum T tracks, through-bolted inboard on the side decks. The main is sheeted at the end of the boom, with the binnacle guard acting as the second attachment point. With this arrangement there is no traveler. In addition to the low-geared, horizontal centerboard winch, five Lewmar winches are provided to handle the sails.

For auxiliary power, the Bristol 35.5 relies on a 24 hp Universal diesel engine with a 2:1 sailing transmission. Westerbeke and Yanmar diesels were also used. Coupled to the standard two-bladed propeller, this power plant supplies a cruising speed of 5.5 knots.

UNDER WAY

The performance under sail of the Bristol 35.5 is quite good. She points well and exhibits very respectable speed on all points of sail. While the C model is tender, as are most centerboarders, it is faster than the deep keeled version. Also, the C model has phenomenal light air performance and great acceleration. It's not necessary to overpower either model with large headsails. A 120 percent or 130 percent jib will do the trick quite well.

BY THE NUMBERS

Ballast/Displacement Ratio ..... (keel/cb) 43%/47%
Displacement/Waterline Length Ratio....... 321.99
Sail Area/Displacement Ratio 15.49
Capsize Screening Ratio...................... 1.76
Motion/Comfort Ratio 32.2

THINGS TO CHECK OUT

It is rare to find significant problems with these boats. However, excluding age-related issues, there are two items that should be kept in mind: The first has to do with the 1977 and early 1978 C models' centerboard. Beware of these. The pendant on these earlier models made three turns and was entirely enclosed, making repairs difficult. Bristol corrected this situation by modifying the centerboard in late 1978.

Second, avoid any boats that are powered by the Yanmar 2QM. That two-cylinder, 20 hp diesel just doesn't have enough power. Look for a boat powered by a Universal or Westerbeke diesel or a three-cylinder equivalent.

OWNER'S COMMENTS

"...ran all the lines back to the cockpit and made it easy for my wife and I to sail the boat shorthanded...the boat was neglected before I got it, part of an estate. I had to replace things that I shouldn't have...no major problems...she's a real head-turner..." Felix E., 1984 model

SUMMING IT UP

The Bristol 35.5 combines quality construction and finish, good sailing performance, and comfortable cruising accommodations in a handsome, traditional package. Bristol 35.5s are always popular and seem to hold their value well. Don't pay extra for a boat with several headsails. Anything more than a 130 percent jib will just overpower the boat. Expect to pay no less than $40,000 for an early model and upwards of $80,000 for a mid '80s version.

"To me, nothing made by man is more beautiful
than a sailboat under way in fine weather,
and to be on that sailboat is to be
as close to heaven as I expect to get."

Robert Manry, *Tinkerbelle,* 1965

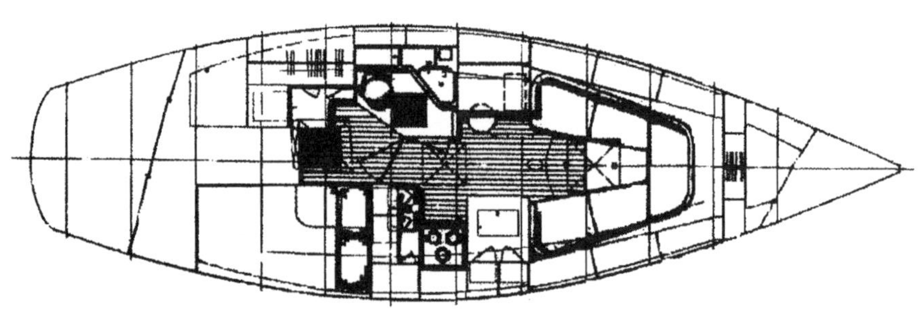

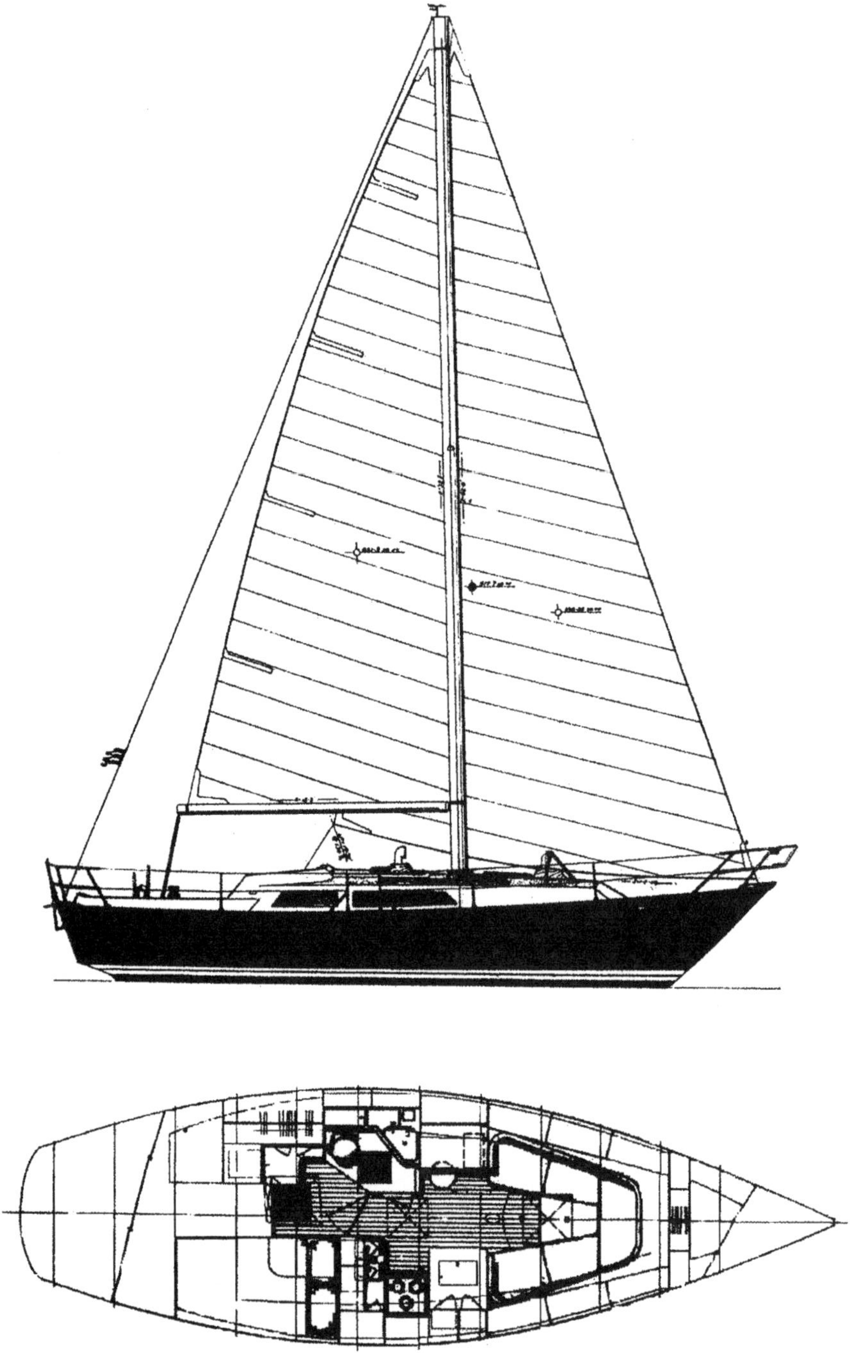

C&C Landfall

C&C LANDFALL 35

The couple's cruiser.

The year was 1961 when George Cuthbertson, a mechanical engineer, and George Cassian, an aircraft designer, got together and formed a partnership with the express intention of building performance sailboats. Cuthbertson managed the business and developed the preliminary lines and calculations, while Cassian dealt with the interior plans and details. The two worked together in a true collaboration. However, it wasn't until George Hinterhoeller, a pair of boatbuilding firms, and a stock broker all got together, that C&C Yachts Ltd. was born. The date was September 26, 1969.

For almost three decades the story of C&C Yachts runs deep and varied, with the ups of numerous technical innovations and successes, both commercially and on the race circuit, the downs of the turbulent '80s, and finally a "fire" sale to Fairport Marine, in 1998.

Throughout its history, C&C's bread and butter was the racer/cruiser, with emphasis on the racer. Of the more than 50 designs, all but a handful fell into this category. That handful was the Landfall series.

Introduced in 1977, the Landfall series was a group of dedicated cruisers targeted for the charter industry. This deviation from C&C's racer/cruiser niche was not entirely successful, even though several models (35, 38, 39, 42, 43, and 48) were produced. The production run of the Landfall series lasted until approximately 1985, at which time C&C returned to their bread and butter, the racer/cruiser.

In 1981, the Landfall 35 appeared; it was manufactured at C&C's Rhode Island facility for five years. Smallest of the Landfalls, the boat was advertised as the "Couple's Cruiser."

She was built with two distinctly different cabin interior arrangements. The first was the traditional V-berth and opposing settee setup, while the second was an entirely new concept: Instead of a V-berth, forward of the mast was a large V-shaped settee with dinette table that converted into a generously large double berth. While the hull, deck, sailing characteristics, and so on are the same for either model, it's the accommodations of the second interior arrangement that makes for a unique cruising yacht.

DESIGN AND CONSTRUCTION

The C&C Landfall 35 is a sloop with a shallow draft fin keel, a partial skeg rudder, and a keel-stepped mast. Its profile is one of a pronounced bow; a smooth, graceful shear; a slightly upswept transom; a wide beam; and a low coach roof. These combined elements translate into one thing: seakeeping ability.

The hull's exterior skin, ¼-inch thick, consists of handlaid fiberglass mat and roving that has been saturated with polyester resin. Beneath a portion of that exterior skin is ½-inch end-grain balsa coring. The coring material is strategically located amidships, at the hull's widest point. It begins at the leading edge of the keel, continues aft, and terminates at the turn of the hull, just forward of the rudder post. Approximately six inches from where the keel box is located, the coring extends out and up and terminates at the waterline. To complete the fabrication, which completely encapsulates the balsa coring, there's an interior skin of ¼-inch fiberglass. Hull thickness in the cored area is one inch. While a balsa cored hull is not without its problems, a properly balsa cored boat exhibits a 50 percent increase in hull strength.

The deck, cabin top, and cockpit sole are solid fiberglass. High stress areas are cored with encapsulated balsa or plywood. All deck hardware is through-bolted. The hull-to-deck joint is bonded and through-bolted every eight inches. Internally, the boat has eight structural bulkheads made of either mahogany or marine plywood, which are either taped or bolted to both the hull and deck. All the plywood is marine grade, encapsulated with epoxy and finished with a final layer of white gelcoat. The cabin sides are covered with vinyl; the headliner is fiberglass.

The ballast, 5,500 pounds of it, is a single lead casting hung externally by eight one-inch stainless steel keel bolts. The partial skeg-hung rudder is comprised of fiberglass over a stainless steel frame and rudder post.

ON DECK

The large foredeck is partially surrounded by a bow pulpit with an integrated teak seat/step. A large rode locker also permits access to the stemhead fitting's fasteners and the bow's hull-to-deck joint bolts. The side decks are 15 inches wide and have a molded-in, 2-inch-tall toe rail, capped with teak. All the footing surfaces are finished in molded-in nonskid.

The cabin top is also serviceable from a seakeeping perspective, for it is wide and has a minimal number of protrusions to get underfoot. Forward is a large (24 inches by 24 inches) smoked plexiglass hatch flanked by a pair of cowl vents with teak Dorade boxes. A stainless steel guard protects these cowl vents. Abaft the mast a slightly smaller center hatch (20 inches by 20 inches) is also flanked by a pair of cowl vents with teak Dorades. There's a small hatch over the head and, on either side, there are teak handrails to aid in on-deck maneuvering. The companionway, offset to port, consists of a sliding, smoked plexiglass hatch with integral spray hood that's designed for use with a dodger. A single mahogany hatch board is used to secure the opening. On the sides of the cabin there are two opening portlights forward and four large smoked fixed ports in the aft section.

The cockpit is larger than one would like for offshore work—it measures 64 inches by 104 inches, has 7-inch-tall coamings, and can easily seat eight adults in reasonable comfort—but that spaciousness does contribute to the quality of living aboard. Just forward of the Edson pedestal steering, the traveler separates the helmsman from the rest of the cockpit. There are four cockpit seat lockers: a large one for sail stowage, a second for propane, and two others for miscellaneous gear. Access to a portion of the boat's mechanical and electrical systems can be obtained via these lockers. A stainless steel stern pulpit with an integrated, centerline swim ladder completes the on-deck picture.

BELOW DECK

The unique layout is designed for a cruising couple to live aboard comfortably. Rather than the standard V-berth, the forward bulkhead is cut to form a large locker with shelves, beneath which is access to the 40-gallon fuel tank. Immediately aft is the main saloon with its very large V-shaped settee. Centered in the settee, a V-shaped table can easily accommodate seven adults. This table is designed to be lowered to fill the center of the V. After the cushions are rearranged and set in place, the space is transformed into a very large, comfortable bed. Beneath the settees is a pair of 32-gallon potable water tanks. Above each settee back is a 7-foot 9-inch shelf; above that are additional stowage bins and compartments. A pair of fixed portlights, the large overhead hatch, and two opening portlights provide illumination and ventilation. Additionally, there are four fluorescent lights recessed behind a teak valance as well as four directional/reading lamps mounted in the overhead liner. A fan helps circulate cabin air.

Aft and to starboard of the V-shaped dinette is the U-shaped galley. This is comprised of twin, deep stainless steel sinks with pressurized and manual water; a large, well insulated icebox; a gimbaled, three-burner alcohol stove with oven; and numerous drawers, cabinets, and cupboards for dry goods and galleyware stowage. It is a very workable galley, even in a somewhat rough seaway.

Directly across from the galley's icebox and to port is the navigation station. It's situated close to amidships and offers a view through the large fixed portlight. The station consists of a three-drawer cabinet, a lift-top chart table, and a swing-out stool.

Both the galley and navigation station are serviced by the second overhead hatch and artificially illuminated by several lights. The galley additionally benefits from a fan. Beneath the teak and holly cabin sole is a relatively deep and long bilge, which allows for access to the keel bolts and mast step, and provides additional stowage space. The head and galley sinks happen to share the same seacock, also located in the bilge.

Aft of the navigation station, the head compartment consists of a molded-in shower with teak grate, the head, a molded-in sink with handheld shower head, a vanity with stowage lockers and clothes hamper, and a bulkhead-mounted mirror with teak trim. There's a fixed portlight, a small overhead hatch, and three lights—but surprisingly, no fan. The compartment is quite roomy and user friendly.

Separating the aft stateroom from the main saloon is a mahogany privacy door. The aft stateroom is divided in two, with the sleeping quarters to starboard and stowage to port.

The stateroom's berth is 6 feet 6 inches long and 48 inches wide at the head. Located beneath is the battery compartment (with space for three batteries), the alcohol tank for the stove, and the holding tank. Outboard and above the berth, a fiddled shelf runs the length of the compartment. Ventilation and illumination are provided by a large fixed portlight, a port that opens to the cockpit footwell, three lights, and a fan.

Opposite the sleeping quarters and on the port side is the aft stateroom's stowage area, which consists of a six-drawer bureau, a large hanging locker (think closet), and a shelf.

Specifications

LOA	34'11"
LWL	26'9"
Beam	10'8"
Draft	4'10"
Displacement	13,000 lbs.
Ballast	5,500 lbs.
Sail Area	545 sq. ft.

The Rig

The C&C Landfall 35 has a bridge clearance of 46 feet from its DWL to the top of its keel-stepped mast. This sloop is masthead rigged with 545 square feet of sail comprised of a Bermudan mainsail and a 135 percent genoa. This gives the boat a sail area/displacement ratio of 15.77. The spars are painted aluminum extrusions with internal sail tracks. All standing rigging was originally stainless steel rod, with the shrouds mounted to outboard chain plates and incorporating a single pair of airfoil spreaders. The halyards are internal and receive mechanical advantage from two mast-mounted Barient winches. The genoa sheets are led aft through cars/tracks situated on the side decks. They terminate at primary Barient winches located on the port and starboard cockpit coamings. The main is end-boom sheeted to a traveler situated just forward of the helm.

For auxiliary power, the Landfall 35 uses a 3-cylinder, 27 hp Yanmar diesel. This engine is freshwater cooled and is installed facing aft; therefore, it relies on a V-drive transmission to transfer power to the propeller. At 2,500 rpms, it moves the boat along at 7 knots. Access to the engine is gained by removing the companionway ladder and the engine hatch. The ability to perform routine maintenance (oil, filter, and impeller) is rated as average or slightly below.

UNDER WAY

Close hauled, the boat will sail to within 50 degrees of true wind; however, her best point of sail is closer to 70 degrees. Some leeway may be experienced. This is attributable to the boat's shallow keel. The boat is fast and accelerates quickly; after all, C&C built it. Weather helm is minimal and the boat will quickly heel to 30 degrees. With all sails up and a stiff breeze, don't be surprised if she approaches >40 degrees of heel. With a ballast/displacement ratio of 42 percent and a capsize screening ratio of 1.82, don't worry: the boat's solid. However, if there is concern, use one or both of the reef points to depower and reduce heel. On a reach, she straightens up somewhat and sails predictably. To sail downwind, the boom may need a helping hand to get it out to the desired location, but once set, steering will be easy and the motion will be predictable with little or no hobbyhorsing.

When backing under power, the boat will tend to pull to port and will be difficult to back to starboard. This is due to the combination of prop walk and the offset propeller shaft. Set the rudder hard to starboard and eventually, once the rudder bites, backing will become more normal.

BY THE NUMBERS

Ballast/Displacement Ratio	42%
Displacement/Waterline Length Ratio	303.2
Sail Area/Displacement Ratio	15.77
Capsize/Screening Ratio	1.82
Motion Comfort Ratio	29.18

THINGS TO CHECK OUT

While cored hulls are strong, they are susceptible to water intrusion and subsequent delamination. Have a certified marine surveyor thoroughly check out the hull. Don't rely solely on moisture meter readings; remove through-hulls. Any additional cost will be worth it.

The engine instrument panel is located low on the bridge deck in the cockpit footwell. If the cockpit has ever been pooped, especially with saltwater, damage may have occurred.

Check for age- and stress-related cracks in the large fixed plexiglass portlights.

The cockpit is large, very large. Consider adding additional drains to help remove water more quickly.

Owner's Comments

"...had to recore about 4 areas on the deck that got soggy and delaminated...the hull is OK, and I plan on keeping it that way. I scooped out the balsa around the through hulls and filled the voids with epoxy...the boat sails well...plenty of room for us and our dog..." Ed S., 1983 model

Summing it Up

It's the accommodations of this boat that truly set it apart from the rest of the pack. Its unique layout is designed for the cruising couple. While it's not a deep draft boat, its overall design equates to seakeeping ability. With proper safety equipment and solid seamanship, the Landfall 35 is capable of sailing to exotic destinations. The cost of a C&C Landfall 35 ranges from $30,000 to $50,000, depending upon condition, equipment, and location.

"Sailing is the second sexiest sport."

Dr. Ruth Westheimer

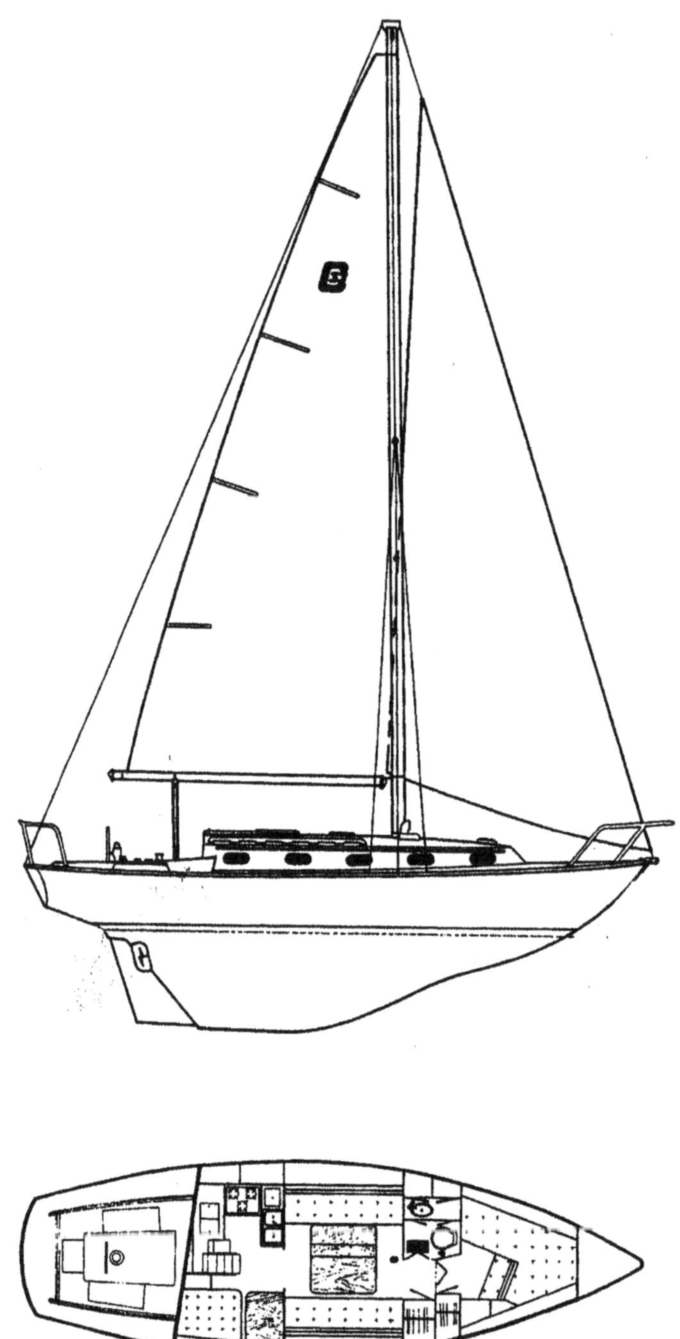

Cape Dory 33

Cape Dory 33

TRADITIONAL, STURDY, AND CONSERVATIVE

Cape Dory Yachts of East Taunton, Massachusetts was founded in 1963 by Andrew Vavolotis. Until its demise 28 years later, the company built over 2,800 sailboats, ranging in length from 18 to 45 feet. It was a conservative firm whose boats had that traditional look. Noted naval architect Carl Alberg was responsible for almost all of the company's designs, including the Cape Dory 33. From his drawing board he espoused full keels with attached rudders, relatively narrow beams, attractive sheer lines, and moderate overhangs.

While other manufacturers began focusing their attention on the racer/cruiser with its fin keel and high aspect ratio rig, Cape Dory continued to stay the course and do what it did best, creating a complete line of conservative sailboats. This tack served the company well. Because Cape Dory produced boats with consistently high quality and excellent resale value, customer loyalty was tremendous.

The Cape Dory 33 was introduced in 1980 and nicely filled the void that existed between the Cape Dory 30 and the much larger and more expensive Cape Dory 36. One hundred and twenty-four Cape Dory 33s were produced between 1980 and 1985. In 1986, after modifying the cockpit and the interior a bit, the company introduced the Cape Dory 330. Only a couple dozen of this model were built between 1986 and 1989.

Around 1991, Cape Dory ceased operations. Its name was sold and most of its designs and molds were scattered among a number of boatmakers.

Some models are still being made, mostly on a semicustom basis. What remained of the company and its marine hardware division, Spartan Marine, went to Maine with Andy Vavolotis. There he started Robinhood Marine and began manufacturing the Robinhood 36 and 40 using the Cape Dory 36 and 40 molds. Several sets of molds, including those for the Cape Dory 33, were sold to Nauset Marine, a custom boatbuilder on Cape Cod.

DESIGN AND CONSTRUCTION

The hull of the Cape Dory 33 is a moderately heavy, solid laminate consisting of polyester resin and alternating layers of fiberglass mat and roving. Structural members encapsulated in fiberglass, full and partial bulkheads, and molded fiberglass liners permanently bonded to the hull all work to support an already stout hull.

The decks and cabin top are constructed of fiberglass and resin and cored with end-grain balsa. The result is a firm, stiff surface with excellent sound and heat insulating properties. Moisture saturation of the balsa core and delamination are common problems, especially around the chain plates and other deck hardware. The quality of the gelcoat is very good.

The hull-to-deck joint is a wide internal flange that is chemically bonded with a semi-rigid polyester compound and reinforced with screws that also attach the toe rail. Secondary mechanical fastening is obtained by the through-bolting of randomly located deck hardware, lifeline stanchions, and the bow and stern pulpits.

The 5,500 pounds of ballast is a lead casting carried in the hollow keel molding. This gives the boat a ballast/displacement ratio of 41 percent. All voids between the casting and keel shell are filled with thickened polyester; the casting is heavily glassed over on the inside of the hull. The Cape Dory 33's rudder is a fiberglass laminate that is hung from the back of the keel by means of a cast bronze gudgeon/heel fitting mounted with silicon bronze fasteners.

Spartan Marine Products, a wholly owned division of Cape Dory, produced all the deck hardware. In keeping with tradition, all deck hardware is bronze and is through-bolted using stainless steel bolts and aluminum backing plates. Although these components are not immersed in an electrolyte, there does exist a difference in electrical potential between the dissimilar metals, especially the bronze and aluminum. This could result in the corrosion of the aluminum backing plates.

On Deck

Whether the boat is rigged as a sloop or as a cutter will determine, for the most part, how much room there is to move about on the foredeck. Side decks are wide; walking surfaces are molded-in nonskid. There is a combination teak toe rail/rail and the shrouds are attached to outboard chain plates.

On the forward portion of the cabin top is an opening hatch followed aft by two cowl vents with teak Dorade boxes. A second opening hatch is situated just forward of the sea hood. Teak handrails, starting at the mast and running aft to the end of the roof, are mounted on either side of the cabin top. Ten bronze, opening portlights capped with teak "eyebrow" accent strips are situated along the cabin's sides.

The cockpit of the Cape Dory 33 is large and can accommodate seven adults. The teak coamings are reasonably high but definitely not comfortable. A bridge deck prevents water from a filled cockpit from cascading below, while a pair of drains located forward on the cockpit sole helps remove water. For stowage there are port and starboard cockpit seat lockers and access to the lazarette beneath the helmsman's seat.

The companionway is offset to starboard. This accomplishes several things: Since the traveler is situated on the bridge deck, an offset companionway often allows for easier maneuvering around the main sheet when crew is coming and going between cockpit and cabin. When transiting canals with the mast unstepped, the mast is secured along the boat's centerline; having the companionway offset makes for easier movement to and from the cabin without the associated head-banging. Finally, from an accommodation point of view, the offset companionway creates more room for the galley.

BELOW DECK

Forward is what some have called the "owner's stateroom." Rather than the standard V-berth configuration, there is an offset L-shaped berth to port and a reading settee to starboard, followed by a bureau and a hanging locker plus shelves located outboard and overhead. A filler piece converts the space into an athwartships double. The forward hatch and a pair of opening portlights service this cabin. For privacy, a bifold wooden door can close this area off from the remainder of the boat.

On the starboard side, just aft of the forward cabin is a second hanging locker with bureau top. Across from this hanging locker, on the port side, is the entrance to the head with its washbasin, vanity, lockers, and shower with teak grate. An opening portlight and a cowl vent with Dorade contribute illumination and ventilation to this compartment.

The main saloon is traditionally styled with port and starboard opposing settees. While the starboard settee functions as a single berth, the port settee easily converts into a double. There is a large centerline drop leaf table. Seven opening portlights, an opening hatch above the table, and a Dorade vent keep the main saloon well lit and well ventilated.

Abaft and to port is the well-equipped and well-appointed U-shaped galley, with its deep double stainless steel sink; large icebox; alcohol stove with oven; and numerous lockers, drawers, bins, and shelves.

To starboard is the forward-facing navigation station and a quarter berth with a full length fiddled shelf. The forward portion of the berth serves as the seat for the chart table.

The Cape Dory 33's warm interior consists of mostly teak and selected hardwoods and a teak and holly sole. White laminate surfaces trimmed in teak are used in the head and galley. This decorative technique brightens up these two areas. Headroom is a generous 6 feet 3 inches.

SPECIFICATIONS

LOA..33'½"
LWL..24'6"
Beam..10'3"
Draft..4'10"
Displacement..................................13,300 lbs.
Ballast..5,500 lbs.
Sail Area....................(sloop/cutter) 539/546 sq. ft.

THE RIG

The Cape Dory 33 was offered as a sloop, with 539 square feet of sail and a sail area/displacement (SA/D) ratio of 15:36, or as a cutter, with 546 square feet of sail and a SA/D ratio of 15:6. In both instances, the mast is keel stepped and supported by a single pair of cap shrouds, dual fore and aft shrouds, a single pair of spreaders, a forestay, and a backstay. Both sloop and cutter are considered medium aspect rigs. The spars are anodized aluminum with internal sail tracks. Bridge clearance is 49 feet. The traveler is mounted on the bridge deck; no fewer than seven bronze Lewmar winches serve the halyards, sheets, and jiffy reefing. Steering is wheel.

Depending upon the year, the Cape Dory was either powered by the 24 hp Universal or the 23 hp Volvo Penta; both marine diesels provide adequate performance. To access the engine for maintenance, one removes the companionway ladder and a cabinet housing the engine. Access is rated as good.

UNDER WAY

The Cape Dory 33 is not a light air boat, but in modest to heavy air she really comes alive. The boat is initially a bit tender; however, at about 15 degrees of heel she stiffens up nicely. The split sail plan of the cutter is advantageous offshore, but the sloop is less complex. The full keel with its attached rudder allows the boat to track well both on and off of the wind. Because of the outboard shrouds, the sheeting angle is somewhat compromised (especially with a big genoa); this may limit how close to the wind the boat can sail. While the boat really enjoys a fresh breeze, when the weather helm gets strong, it's time to shorten the sail.

BY THE NUMBERS

Ballast/Displacement Ratio.....................41 percent
Displacement/Waterline Length Ratio..............403:74
Sail Area/Displacement Ratio...(sloop/cutter)15:36/15:6
Capsize Screening Ratio................................1:73
Motion Comfort Ratio...............................33:98

THINGS TO CHECK OUT

The deck and cabin top of the Cape Dory 33 are cored with end-grain balsa. It is quite common for the core to become saturated with water, resulting in delamination. Sound out the areas around all deck fittings, especially the chain plates.

There have also been reports of rudders becoming saturated and delaminated. Another problem is osmotic blistering of the hull. In some cases it has been moderate to severe.

The company used mild steel as the attachment point for the lower shrouds' chain plates, where water seepage has resulted in significant corrosion. Because of the bonded hull liner, these areas are difficult to inspect.

All deck hardware is bronze and through-bolted to aluminum backing plates with stainless steel bolts. There is a difference in electrical potential between these dissimilar metals. Check out the condition of the backing plates.

Only two relatively small drains serve the cockpit. Consider enlarging them or adding an additional pair aft.

OWNER'S COMMENTS

"...example of another outstanding Carl Alberg design...can handle just about anything Mother Nature and Neptune can throw her way... replaced the rudder that split apart...since I barrier coated the hull, no blistering...we are both schoolteachers, so we move aboard each summer and cruise..."

Nick H., 1983 model

SUMMING IT UP

The Cape Dory 33, rigged either as a sloop or a cutter, is easily driven, responsive, and very stable. It is a conservatively designed and solidly constructed offshore cruiser. Below-deck inspection reveals a boat that stands apart from most production sailboats. Its mostly wood interior is warm and inviting. The boat is not without deficiencies; however, corrective actions and upgrades won't break the bank and the boat is worth it. The price of a Cape Dory 33 can range from $40,000 for a 1980 model to near $60,000 for one built in 1985.

"To reach the port of heaven, we must sail
sometimes with the wind and sometimes against it,
but we must sail, and not drift, nor lie at anchor."

Oliver Wendell Holmes

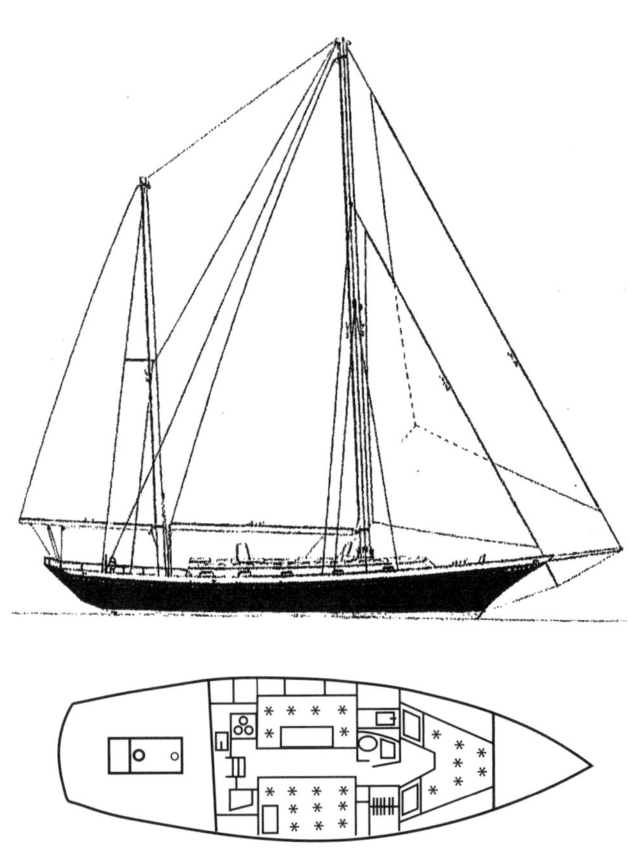

Cheoy Lee Clipper 36

CHEOY LEE CLIPPER 36

A classic blue-water cruiser from Asia.

Prior to the advent of fiberglass construction, Cheoy Lee Shipyards of Hong Kong was producing a variety of wooden, commercial watercraft at their Kowloon waterfront facility. The same family had run Cheoy Lee Shipyards since 1870 and had developed a reputation for quality workmanship. They also enjoyed a large labor pool and favorably low labor rates. The incentive to buy Asian was well established. And when the transition from wood to fiberglass began in the early 1960s, Cheoy Lee became one of the pioneers of fiberglass/foam sandwich technology in the marine field. Almost immediately, several North American designers commissioned Cheoy Lee to produce some of their designs in fiberglass. The list of naval architects includes such names as Perry, Pedrick, Rhodes, Alden, and Luders, to name but a few.

A. E. "Bill" Luders, Jr. was a major contributor to the Cheoy Lee product line. Nearly a dozen designs came from his drawing board. He was responsible for many of the Midshipman series of boats, some of the Offshore series, and all of the Clipper series.

The Clipper series included the 33, 36, 42, and 48. Most were rigged as cutter ketches, with a Yankee, staysail, main, and a mizzen. All were heavy displacement boats, designed as cruisers, and built exactly to Lloyds 100A1 specifications.

The Clipper 36 was in production from 1969 to around 1988, during which time approximately 70 hulls were produced. It was eventually eclipsed and subsequently replaced by the Pedrick 36, which was of a more contemporary design.

The Clipper 36 is a classic blue-water yacht. Many have crossed oceans and many are being refitted to continue to sail the world. So if you're looking for a character cruiser that's ready to sail the seven seas, you'll fall hard for this Bill Luders beauty.

By the way, following the 1997 Chinese takeover of Hong Kong, Cheoy Lee relocated their facilities to a much larger and more modern site located on the Pearl River, 60 miles from Hong Kong, at Doumen, China. Today, Cheoy Lee Shipyards makes everything from ferries to 144-foot motor yachts. Their current sailboat lineup includes a 53-footer, a 63-footer, a 78-foot motorsailer, and a 77-foot pilothouse cutter.

DESIGN AND CONSTRUCTION

A graceful sheer, moderate overhangs, a clipper bow with bowsprit, and wooden spars exemplify the Clipper 36's classic lines. It is a very heavy displacement boat with a high displacement/waterline length ratio of 464. The underwater lines of the Clipper 36 reveal a very traditional Y shape with a full keel and attached rudder.

Its hull is handlaid solid fiberglass that ranges in thickness from one inch at the keel to approximately 7/16 inch at the sheer. The deck is also a fiberglass laminate; most were overlaid with 3/8-inch teak.

The rudder is a fiberglass sandwich cored with foam. It is mounted onto the aft edge of the keel, and rides on a cast bronze heel fitting. The 5,375 pounds of ballast is in the form of cast iron that has been externally fitted to the keel. This gives the boat a ballast/displacement ratio of 33 percent.

The interior is all Burmese teak and the joinery is superb. All of the bulkheads are tabbed to the hull, which makes for a strong and cohesive craft. Tankage, of fiberglass construction, consists of a 100-gallon potable water tank and a 60-gallon fuel tank.

ON DECK

A stainless steel pulpit surrounds the wooden bowsprit. This affords a much-needed degree of safety, especially when working forward under adverse conditions. Except for a Sampson post and a deck pipe, both of which are located forward, the foredeck is expansive. It's all business and offers room for a windlass, stowage of a hard dinghy, or a good place to catch some rays, if you're so inclined. The side decks are wide and are surrounded by high bulwarks. Add to this outboard shrouds and a teak handrail that runs the length of the cabin top, and fore and aft movement is made both relatively easy and safe.

On the cabin top, there's a forward hatch followed aft by a pair of cowl vents with Dorades, a teak and Plexiglass skylight, and finally the seahood for the sliding companionway hatch. There are ten portlights situated along the cabin's sides; all were originally fixed.

The cockpit is generous enough, has a large footwell, and is surrounded by a wooden taffrail supported by turned spindles. There are no coamings to keep water out or with which to brace oneself. Located beneath the port cockpit seat is a sail bin and beneath the bridge deck, a locker for gas bottle stowage. Steering is by wheel via cable/quadrant. Surprisingly, there are no provisions for an emergency tiller. The companionway is offset to starboard in order to circumvent the mizzenmast.

The decking, including the cockpit seating area, is overlaid with teak.

BELOW DECK

While the headroom is over 6 feet, the interior of the Clipper 36 is on the smallish side. With the exception of the white headliner that is battened with teak strips, the two-cabin arrangement of the Clipper 36 is comprised entirely of varnished Burmese teak.

Just aft of the chain locker in the forepeak is the forward cabin with its V-berth and filler. A pair of fiddled shelves outboard and above as well as lockers beneath the berth provide forward stowage. Ventilation and illumination are by means of the forward opening hatch and a pair of fixed portlights.

A hanging locker is to starboard, while the head compartment—with stainless steel sink, shower, and vanity with hamper—is to port. A pair of Dorade ventilators and a pair of fixed portlights provide light and air movement.

The main cabin is available in two layouts, offering subtle differences. Layout A features a convertible dinette to port with a shelf behind and a hinged pilot berth to starboard with a settee and drawers beneath. Layout B is quite traditional and predictable. It features a centerline drop leaf table, port and starboard opposing settees with drawers beneath, and port and starboard hinged pilot berths. In both cases an overhead skylight and six fixed portlights provide illumination.

The galley spans the aft portion of the main cabin, with the three-burner gimbaled stove with oven to port, a stainless steel sink almost on the centerline, and an icebox that doubles as a chart table to starboard. The arrangement is quite workable and offers plenty of stowage for dry goods and galleyware in several lockers, bins, and drawers.

A wet locker located just aft of the icebox and convenient to the companionway completes the picture. Access to the engine is behind/ beneath the companionway stairs.

SPECIFICATIONS

LOA	35'7"
LWL	25'
Beam	10'9"
Draft	5'3'
Displacement	16,250 lbs.
Ballast	5,375 lbs.
Sail Area	635 sq. ft.

THE RIG

Most Clipper 36s were rigged as cutter ketches, with a Yankee, staysail, main, and a mizzen. This equates to a sail area of 635 square feet and a sail area/displacement ratio of 15.84. There were also a couple of boats that were rigged as schooners. Both the main and mizzen masts are stepped on deck. All spars are hollow and constructed of Sitka spruce. The masts each incorporate a single pair of spreaders, and their shrouds are attached to outboard chain plates. The main originally came standard with roller reefing, the mizzen with slab. Halyard winches are mounted on the masts and sheeting is end-boom for both main and mizzen. Headsail controls consist of tracks located either on the bulwarks or outboard on the side decks for the Yankee, and on the coach roof for the staysail. The primary winches flank the cockpit; the secondaries are on the aft edge of the coach roof.

There was a choice of auxiliary power, either gasoline (Atomic 4) or diesel (Westerbeke 4-107 or Perkins 4-108). All of the engines are highly reliable; however, access for maintenance is terrible.

UNDER WAY

Owing to its relatively narrow beam and Y-shaped hull, the Clipper 36 is initially tender, but stiffens up nicely at about 15 degrees of heel. The boat's divided sail plan enables her to be easily balanced; her seakeeping ability is excellent. The Clipper 36's motion comfort ratio is a comfortable 37.43, while her capsize screening ratio is a low 1.70. The boat's best point of sail is on a reach. While on a run or going to weather she's a bit slower.

Regardless of the auxiliary, expect the boat to make about 6 knots in relatively calm seas. Backing up under power is another story. Like all boats with full keels, attached rudders, and a propeller in an aperture, the Clipper 36 does not track well in reverse.

BY THE NUMBERS

Ballast/Displacement Ratio	33%
Displacement/Waterline Length Ratio	464.29
Sail Area/Displacement Ratio	15.84
Capsize Screening Ratio	1.70
Motion Comfort Ratio	37.43

THINGS TO CHECK OUT

While the company had a reputation for superior workmanship, some of their boats suffered from problems endemic to Asia, such as substandard electrical and metal work. Also, like many Asian builders, Cheoy Lee produced many of its own parts. This became an area of concern, and during the 1980s, customers began to demand brand-name accessories and not "cheap Asian knock-offs." Not to worry: by now most Clipper 36s have gone through an owner or two and the boats' more glaring weaknesses have been addressed.

While the boat's interior is quite complex and access to her systems is not always easy or straightforward, a good survey is a must. Pay particular attention to the following areas:

- Leaking skylight
- Chain plate corrosion
- Electrical wiring and electrical components
- Mixed metallurgy
- Poor quality castings
- Corrosion of the cast iron ballast
- Integrity of the teak decks
- Engine (because access for maintenance is so bad)
- Wooden spars (especially if painted)

OWNERS' COMMENTS

"...lots of nice teak work below...solidly built...engine and stuffing box hard to access...very satisfied with boat to date..." Jim M., 1969 model

"...with her Sitka spruce masts and seemingly acres of teak, it is sometimes a daunting task to keep her varnish good looking...the sails are small and easily handled by one or two people...overall construction is very rugged and gives you a feeling of confidence...original stainless steel fittings and chain plates were made from inferior grade metal and most owners have replaced these items...the cast iron ballast keel needs to be tended to every couple of years...we have been living aboard since the spring of 2002...I am not sure that we could be any happier with her..." Jamie S., 1970 model

SUMMING IT UP

Built to Lloyds' exacting standards, the Cheoy Lee Clipper 36 is a classic blue-water cruising yacht. She is known not for her speed or ease of maintenance, but for her seaworthiness and especially her beauty. The price for good looks is high maintenance, but the reward is the envy of fellow sailors. Depending upon year, condition, and equipment, expect to pay $40,000-$60,000 for a mid to late '70s Clipper 36.

"Until you do it all yourself,
you cannot have any idea of the innumerable minutiae
to be attended to in the proper care of a yacht."

John MacGregor

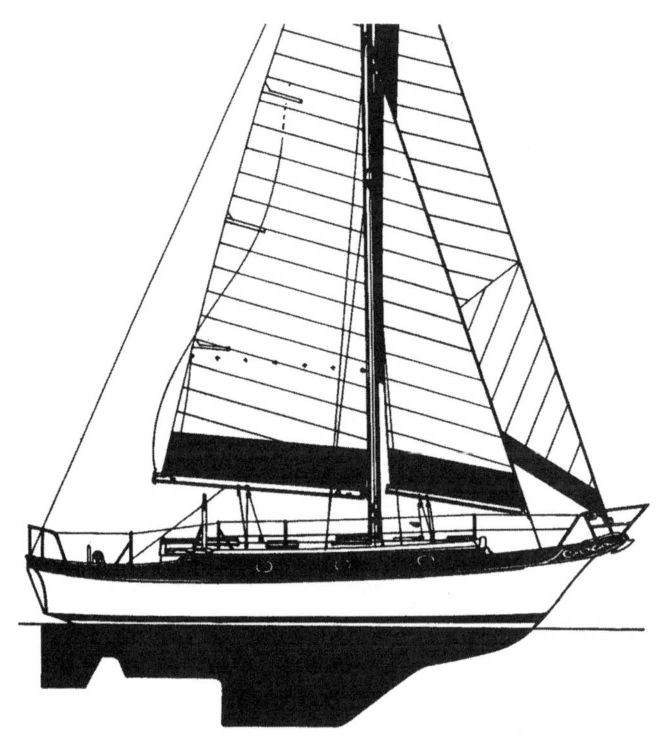

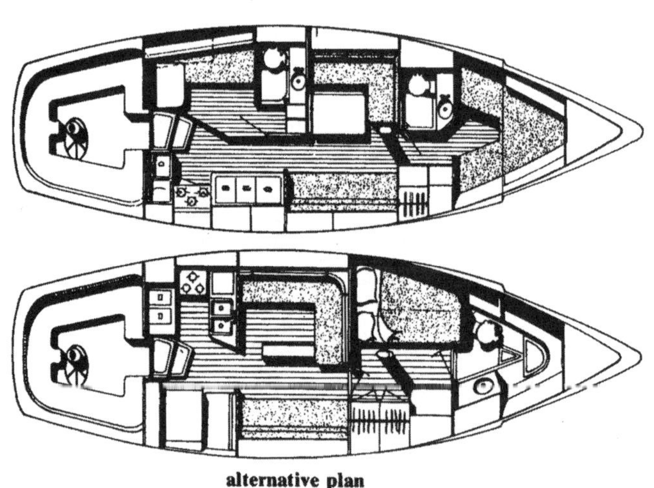

alternative plan

CSY 37

CSY 37

A "bulletproof" cruiser designed to survive the charter service.

Caribbean Sailing Yachts, Limited (CSY, Ltd.) was founded in 1967 in Essex, Connecticut. As its name implies, it operated primarily in the Caribbean, to where it soon physically relocated and expanded. The company started with a fleet of 14 identical production boats. This allowed them to maintain a full set of spares and standardize their operating procedures. By the 1970s CSY, Ltd. had become the largest charter company in the world. This success demanded not only an enlarged fleet, but also a well-built one.

Their next boats were designed and built especially for them by Pearson Yachts. Additional craft were designed by Halsey Herreshoff and manufactured by Bristol Yachts. These new boats brought their fleet up to 85 yachts. Irwin Yacht Corporation was also contracted to build boats for CSY, Ltd., but they never delivered. By the mid-1970s CSY, Ltd., dissatisfied with the boats they were getting, decided that they themselves could design and build boats that could take the punishment that years of charter service routinely dished out.

On September 1, 1976, CSY Yacht Corporation (CSY, Inc.) was founded and was soon building boats in its 64,000-square-foot Tampa, Florida facility. While CSY, Inc. primarily built boats for CSY, Ltd., they did build boats for other charter companies and individuals as well. However, their product line was limited. Their main boat was a 44-foot center cockpit walkover cutter that bears a striking similarity to an Irwin of that size and era. This was followed by a 44-foot pilothouse cutter and finally a 44-foot center cockpit walkthrough cutter. By 1978, CSY, Inc. was the sixth largest sailboat manufacturer in the United States. That same year, a 33-foot cutter and the CSY 37 were introduced.

To add versatility to their line without adding another hull size, CSY, Inc. redesigned the interior of the CSY 37. It was soon available in two configurations: the original two-stateroom model designed for the charter service, and a one-stateroom version popular with individual owners. Production of the CSY 37 continued until 1982, with a total of 87 boats being produced.

Around 1980, CSY, Inc. discovered that they had been selling boats significantly below cost. In an attempt to recoup lost revenue and improve cash flow, they concocted some sort of pyramid scheme, relying on the fact that most of their boats went into their charter fleet after someone else had paid for them. In 1982 CSY went out of business, with a host of lawsuits pending.

While the company may not have been bulletproof, the CSY 37 definitely is. The craft's proven ability to stand up to the constant use and abuse of the charter trade is a credit to both the designer and the builder.

Design and Construction

For CSY, the design and construction of charter yachts became a science; the CSY 37 is a good example of this science being applied. Its overall design is credited to Peter Schmitt, CSY Incorporated's vice-president of engineering and design. The boat is a raised deck cutter with modified keel that carries a modest basic sail plan. A few design features of note include: molded-in trail boards and rubbing strake, the use of a bustle for the protection and support of the prop shaft and propeller, and an unusual convertible keel.

The boat has an immensely strong solid fiberglass hull and deck. No coring materials are used anywhere. The hull was molded in two sections and then joined together down the centerline with numerous overlapping layers of fiberglass mat and roving. Hull thickness varies from 1¼ inches near the keel to 5/8 inch at the turn of the bilge and finally 13/16 along the topsides. The hull-to-deck joint is comprised of overlapping hull and deck flanges which, when chemically bonded with polyurethane and mechanically fastened with stainless steel machine screws on 4-inch centers, form a molded-in rail that is then capped with teak.

The construction of the keel is quite novel. The lowest 16 inches of the keel is filled with approximately 600 pounds of concrete. This concrete-filled section is then heavily glassed over, and close to 8,000 pounds of ballast, in the form of lead, is encapsulated directly above. The result is the deep keel version CSY 37. If a shoal draft boat is desired, the concrete extension is simply cut off.

The rudder, positioned as far aft as possible for good maneuverability, is skeg hung and features a two-inch solid bronze rudder post and cast bronze heel fitting.

All interior bulkheads are marine-grade plywood and are firmly attached to the hull. Airex pads are situated along the outer edges to distribute the loading on the hull and eliminate any hard spots.

On Deck

The stainless steel stemhead fitting is massive and incorporates an anchor roller, a chock, and the headstay chain plate. A stainless steel pulpit that smoothly leads to high foredeck bulwarks surrounds the boat's prominent bow and a recessed anchor locker. This arrangement makes for a protected foredeck.

The boat's raised deck, situated amidships, offers a considerable amount of cabin top deck space for passenger movement, on-deck stowage, or placement of hardware.

On the cabin top there are five opening hatches made of molded fiberglass with translucent panels and one opening skylight, all of which appear to have good gasketing and latches. Located forward of the mast is the traveler for the clubfooted staysail. The traveler for the main is also situated on the cabin top, just forward of the sea hood for the companionway's sliding hatch.

The cockpit of the CSY 37 is just what you would expect for the charter trade: big. It is self-bailing by means of four large drains, but it lacks a bridge deck, and the companionway sill is a tad low. These areas need to be addressed before venturing too far off shore. High coamings give occupants the secure feeling of being down in. For the helmsman, there's a contoured helm seat. There are port and starboard cockpit seat lockers for stowage. Both are large, well divided, and partitioned from the engine. The boat's batteries are housed in the starboard locker. The cockpit sole is, for the most part, a large, heavy, sound-insulating hatch that provides excellent access to the engine.

All deck hardware is through-bolted and incorporates backing plates.

BELOW DECK

The CSY 37 is available in two interior arrangements: the original two-stateroom model designed for the charter trade, and a single-stateroom version that is well laid out for liveaboard use. For a seafaring couple, a CSY 37 with what is referred to as the alternate plan would be the more desirable of the two interior layouts.

In place of the traditional forward V-berth, the alternate plan features a reasonably spacious head compartment, as well as stowage. Compliments of the raised deck, there is standing headroom in this compartment. Abaft the head is the single stateroom, with a double berth to port and a bureau and his-and-her hanging lockers to starboard. The keel-stepped mast is prominently located here, but it doesn't appear to be a hindrance in moving about. In fact, it just might be useful in preventing someone from falling out of the berth.

A privacy door separates the forward stateroom and head from the main saloon. An L-shaped dinette with a fixed centerline drop leaf table is to port, and a single settee is to starboard. By swinging the back of the starboard settee inward and up and latching it into place, one can form a pair of bunk berths. All berths are a generous 6 feet 6 inches. Stowage cabinets and bookshelves are located outboard and above both the dinette and starboard settee.

Completing the main saloon is a navigation station with a spacious chart table to starboard and the U-shaped galley to port. In the galley there is a deep double stainless steel sink with both pressurized hot and cold water and a manual potable water foot pump; a gimbaled, three burner, propane cooktop with oven; and a well insulated two-bin icebox. Commonly found upgrades may include either 110-VAC refrigeration or engine-driven refrigeration designed by Crosby.

A removable three-step spiral stairway gives forward access to the engine compartment. The boat carries 20 gallons of water and 50 gallons of diesel.

Because of the raised deck and 12-foot beam, the boat's interior volume is huge. Ventilation and illumination are superb, with the numerous hatches being supplemented by eleven opening, elliptical, screened, bronze portlights. The counters are a plastic laminate, the cabin sole is teak and holly, and the bulkheads may be teak veneer, faced with oak or painted white and trimmed with solid wood. In any event, headroom is well over 6 feet.

SPECIFICATIONS

LOA	37'3"
LWL	29'2"
Beam	12'0"
Draft	(shoal/deep) 4'8"/6'2"
Displacement	19,689 lbs.
Ballast	8,000 lbs.
Sail Area	610 sq. ft.

THE RIG

The CSY 37 is available in two keel configurations and two rigs, the standard short rig and a tall rig that is about 8 feet taller and incorporates two sets of spreaders.

In both instances, the mast is keel stepped and the standing rigging consists of a headstay; a split backstay; and pairs of upper, intermediate, and fore and aft lower shrouds. The spars are aluminum extrusions painted white. The chain plates are located outboard and are responsible for the wide sheeting angles. To eliminate the need for running backstays, the intermediate and aft lower shrouds are attached to chain plates located several feet aft of the mast and the upper shrouds. When on a broad reach or a run, the boom and mainsail make contact with these shrouds.

The CSY 37 carries 610 square feet of sail area comprised of a Yankee, a staysail, and a main. This combination gives the boat a sail area to displacement ratio of 13.39. The three halyard winches, Barient #8s, are located on the mast and/or on the aft cabin top. The Yankee is sheeted on a pair of Barient #27 self-tailing winches located on the teak-capped cockpit coamings. The staysail is clubfooted and sheeted to a traveler mounted on the cabin top just aft of the forward hatch. The main is sheeted mid-boom and is connected to a traveler situated on the cabin top just forward of the sea hood. Keeping in tune with the charter trade, the boom does not extend over the cockpit, there's a teak boom gallows, and steering is wheel.

A 40 hp Westerbeke diesel coupled to a Walters V-drive was the standard auxiliary power. However, some boats were fitted with the Perkins 4-108 diesel. Either engine is adequate.

UNDER WAY

With a displacement-to-waterline length ratio of 354.13, this is a fairly heavy boat. The combination of the heavy displacement, the 12-foot beam, and the short rig makes her a very stiff yacht. While the tall rig will enhance the boat's light air performance, it will also increase the boat's tenderness. It's the shorter rig that will allow the yacht to maintain full working sails to about 20 knots apparent wind with ease. Above that, with the Yankee doused, the boat will balance out and sail well under main and staysail. On the other hand, the tall rig will become overpowered at around 15 knots and will need to be reefed.

To weather, with the shoal keel, the boat does make noticeable leeway, especially in a stiff breeze. By taking a tuck in the main, the boat will stand up and the leeway will be lessened. The deep keel version will noticeably reduce leeway as well as help the boat point better. Off the wind, the boat comes into her own and, assuming that sufficient chafe protection from those aft-placed shrouds is in place, is ready to take on the trade winds.

CSY 37's ballast-to-displacement ratio is 41 percent and her capsize screening ratio is 1.78. Keeping in mind that this yacht was designed for charter service, where comfort is of paramount importance, it's not surprising that the CSY 37's motion comfort ratio is almost 35. When selecting a CSY 37, the least desirable combination would be the tall rig and shoal keel.

Either the Westerbeke or the Perkins is normally adequate to move the boat about. However, the combination of the boat's high topsides, a crosswind, and slow speeds can make maneuvering exciting. Also, reverse under power is a bit tricky.

By the Numbers

Ballast/Displacement Ratio	41%
Displacement/Waterline Length Ratio	354.13
Sail Area/Displacement Ratio	13.39
Capsize Screening Ratio	1.78
Motion Comfort Ratio	34.93

THINGS TO CHECK OUT

While there are no known glaring deficiencies associated with the CSY 37, age-related problems will no doubt be in evidence: these include but are not limited to gelcoat cracks and crazing, worn-out rigging, tired and UV-damaged sails, soiled cushion fabrics, and hardware in need of rebedding.

Since many of these yachts were used in the charter trade, carefully investigate those areas prone to damage due to abuse or inexperienced skippers. A few of the more important areas include the keel and keel bolts, the rudder and rudder post, the stemhead fitting, and the engine.

Don't necessarily disregard a former charter craft. Bear in mind that these boats were designed and built by a charter company specifically for use in charter service. Also, any boat that was out of service or not functioning properly wasn't producing an income. Therefore it's reasonable to say that not only are these boats built to last, but also they more than likely received scheduled routine maintenance.

OWNER'S COMMENTS

"...the 37 is built heavily, but sails nicely...for a couple, it is perfect... mine is a shoal and I have no complaints about her windward abilities... huge cockpit could hold a lot of water if breaking waves board...all in all, if you plan on extensive cruising, I don't think you could be disappointed..." Ian J., 1979 model

SUMMING IT UP

This tubby-looking, high-sided boat is one overbuilt yacht. She'll be comfortable in a rough seaway, but don't expect sparkling performance. Depending upon configuration, the vast interior can be a bit chopped up, but at the same time quite useable. Most boats on the used market will be equipped with all sorts of goodies including refrigeration, a windlass, and a bimini.

The cost of a CSY 37 will range from $48,000 for a '78 model to $65,000 for a 1980 version. Unless a survey reveals major damage, the boat is worth the money.

"Those who travel fastest see the least,
but he that would see, feel, and hear the most
of life, nature, and God,
let him go down to the sea in a small sailing vessel."

L. Francis Herreshoff

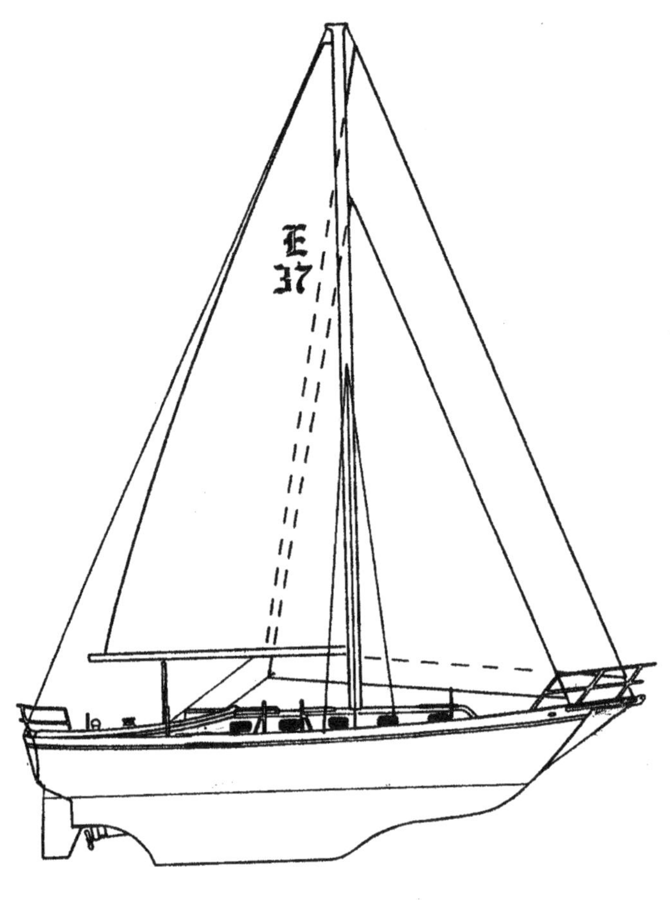

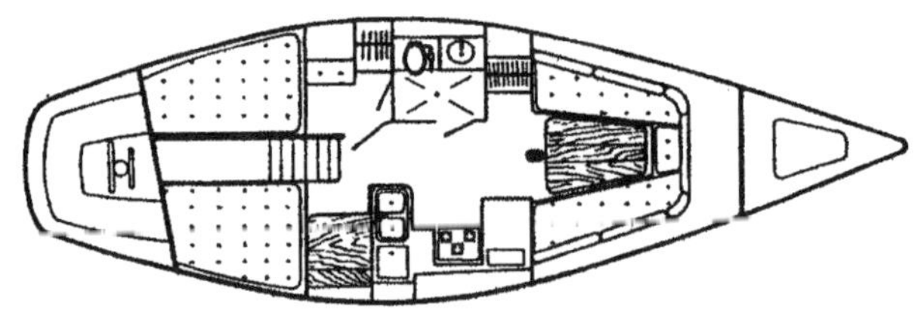

Endeavour 37

ENDEAVOUR 37

A heavily built, nicely finished, comfortable cruising boat of the Florida design.

In 1974 Rob Valdez and John Brooks combined forces and founded the Endeavour Yacht Corporation. They set up shop in the west coast Florida city of Largo. Having met while working at Gulfstar in St. Petersburg, neither Rob nor John was new to the industry. In fact, Rob had previous experience at Columbia Yachts, while John had worked with both Charley Morgan and Ted Irwin.

To help jumpstart the company, Ted Irwin provided Endeavour with a set of molds for a 1970 Irwin 32. After Endeavour's in-house designer Dennis Robbins modified them, this fledgling company launched its first entry into the marketplace, the Endeavour 32. The boat was a success and about 600 were built.

Wanting to capitalize on this success, Rob and John began searching for a sister ship. They discovered an old 34-foot Ray Creekmore design that they thought had possibilities. The talents of Dennis Robbins were again put to work. The 34-foot design was cut in half, three feet were added to the boat's midsection, and the resulting boat was christened the Endeavour 37. The boat, introduced in 1977, continued in production until 1983. During that time a total of 476 boats were sold.

Dennis Robbins soon left Endeavour to work for Ted Irwin. Bob Johnson (founder of Island Packet) took his place and became the principle in-house designer. He spent about three years at Endeavour. Later designs were drawn by Bruce Kelly as well as America's Cup designer John Valentijn.

In 1986 John Brooks sold the company to Coastal Financial Corporation of Denver and stayed on as product manager. Despite the company's upgraded designs and construction methods, sales declined. Competition with its own products on the used boat market effectively put Endeavour Yacht Corporation out of business in 1988.

DESIGN AND CONSTRUCTION

As the story goes, Rob and John were looking for boats along the Miami River when they found the abandoned 34-foot Creekmore design. By lengthening the hull with a three-foot midsection addition, they dramatically changed the basic hull design. This gave the boat a more spacious interior, especially since the expansion took place at the boat's widest part. It also affected the hull's waterline plane when heeled, impacting the boat's ability to balance well.

The Endeavour 37 is a good example of 1970s fiberglass boatbuilding technology: simple and straightforward. The hull is a solid fiberglass laminate consisting of a combination of polyester resin, fiberglass woven roving, and multi-directional chopped strand fiber (MCSF). The decks, cabin top, and cockpit sole are fiberglass laminate sandwiches cored with plywood.

The shoal draft keel is long and is integral to the hull mold. During construction, the 8,000 pounds of lead ballast is lowered into the keel sump and then glassed over. By encapsulating the ballast, there are no keel bolts to contend with.

The long straight run of the keel should take to the bottom well, whether it's an intentional careening or an accidental grounding. After either event, an inspection of the outer skin for damage is prudent. Should a break occur and water enter the keel cavity, the laminate must be thoroughly dried out before repairs can be made.

The spade rudder, a foam-cored fiberglass laminate, is positioned as far aft as possible for good maneuverability.

The boat's interior is plywood either veneered with or trimmed in varnished teak. Workmanship is rated as being good to very good. The

Endeavour 37 was offered in two interior configurations. The A plan featured an aft master suite, popular with liveaboards, while the B plan, with its V-berth, was designed for the charter trade.

ON DECK

The Endeavour 37 is equipped with a bowsprit surrounded by a stainless steel bow pulpit. Its foredeck, although relatively narrow, is adequate for handling sails and ground tackle. Side decks are generously wide and unrestricted. The shrouds are outboard and the toe rail rises slightly as it runs forward. A nonskid deck pattern, cabin-top teak handrail, and dual lifelines add on-deck security.

Evenly spaced along the cabin's sides are ten opening portlights and on the cabin top are three opening hatches.

The large cockpit is surrounded by a high, wide coaming that actually extends forward of the sea hood. It's attractively capped with varnished teak and conveniently houses a cleverly hidden and easily accessed gas bottle locker. In addition to providing excellent back support, the wraparound coaming imparts a strong sense of security. Other nifty cockpit amenities include an insulated beverage cooler and a small trash bin.

While the cockpit might be considered borderline too large for blue-water work, it does have a good bridge deck and a pair of drains. The addition of more or larger scuppers would be a prudent upgrade.

BELOW DECK

The interior of the Endeavour 37 is available in two configurations. Primarily designed for the liveaboard, plan A is a departure from the traditional in that it dispenses with the V-berth. In its place is stowage and lots of it, including an athwartships shelf that is handy for books, bric-a-brac, and possibly a TV or compact stereo.

The large forepeak is divided in two, with one compartment designed as a rode locker and the other intended for sail stowage. Both are accessible from the deck.

Immediately aft is a large U-shaped dinette that can easily accommodate seven for dinner. Lowering the centerline drop leaf table and rearranging the cushions provides a generous double berth. Lying back, one can view the heavens through the large overhead forward hatch.

Amidships and to starboard is the U-shaped galley. A dual stainless steel sink with pressurized hot and cold water plus a foot pump; a three-burner alcohol stove and oven; a side-loading refrigerator; and numerous bins, drawers, and lockers for galleyware and provisions make up the boat's culinary amenities.

Across from the galley on the port side is the door to the head. Standard equipment includes pressurized hot and cold water, a shower with an automatic sump pump, a porcelain sink, and a full-length mirror. A second door leads aft to the private master stateroom. The forward portion is a changing area with a hanging locker and a bureau, plus a door leading to the main cabin. Aft of the changing area and beneath the cockpit is a double berth. Ventilation and natural illumination for this cabin is provided by the combination of an overhead hatch and opening portlights in both the cabin's sides and the cockpit footwell.

Across from the master stateroom on the starboard side is the navigation station, followed aft by a double quarter berth. Without rearranging the U-shaped dinette, plan A easily berths four, six with the dinette converted.

The plan B configuration is quite traditional. The forepeak houses a rode locker (no forward sail stowage) followed by a V-berth. To starboard is a bureau and hanging locker, while to port is the head. In the main saloon is a pair of port and starboard settees and offset drop leaf table. While the port settee pulls out to form a double berth, the hinged backrest of the starboard settee swings up and outboard to form a pilot berth.

Continuing aft and to starboard is the galley that's arranged in an L-shape. In place of the side-loading refrigerator is a 10-cubic-foot top-loading icebox. Counter space and stowage is slightly less that that of plan A.

Across from the galley on the port side is a large chart table followed aft by a double quarter berth. Having the ability to berth eight, it is quite apparent that plan B was designed for charter service.

Both configurations afford 6'6" headroom and sport varnished teak interiors, as well as Endeavour's trademark teak parquet sole throughout.

SPECIFICATIONS

LOA	37'5"
LWL	30'
Beam	11'7"
Draft	4'6"
Displacement	21,000 lbs.
Ballast	8,000 lbs.
Sail Area	(sloop/ketch) 580/640 sq. ft.

THE RIG

The Endeavour 37 came standard as a sloop rig or optionally as a ketch. Sail area for the sloop is 580 square feet; the ketch's sail area is 640 square feet. In both cases, the spars are anodized aluminum extrusions, with the keel-stepped main mast affording a bridge clearance of 46 feet, from DWL. Standing rigging consists of a headstay, a backstay, and upper and dual lower shrouds incorporating single spreaders. When the boat is rigged as a ketch, the mizzenmast penetrates the cockpit sole just forward of the binnacle.

A winch for the main halyard and one for the headsail are mast-mounted. The headsail sheets are led to tracks and cars situated on the rail. Two primary winches are mounted on the wide cockpit coamings. The main is sheeted to a traveler located on the bridge deck. Pedestal steering is standard.

For auxiliary power, the Endeavour 37 is fitted with a freshwater-cooled, 50 hp 4-108 Perkins diesel coupled to a Warner hydraulic gearbox, with a 2.57:1 reduction, which turns a two-blade fixed propeller. This combination does a great job. Fuel capacity is 55 gallons. The engine is situated in a soundproof compartment to which access—rated as good—is gained by removing the companionway steps. Backing elicits the usual complaints.

UNDER WAY

Make no mistake, the Endeavour 37 is a cruising sailboat. With a sail area/displacement ratio of around 12.2, the sloop is definitely underpowered. The ketch rig bumps the ratio up to around 13.5, but in neither case is the boat fast, nor was it designed to be. It's a heavy boat with a displacement/waterline length ratio of close to 350. Despite the boat's fairly fine entry, the outboard chain plates and long shoal keel limit sheeting angles and inhibit the boat from pointing high. Also, above 20 knots the boat develops weather helm and could benefit from a tuck in the main. For light air, a nylon drifter would be a good addition to the sail inventory. This is a cruising boat of the Florida design, where shoal draft is selected over windward performance. (Shallow draft is a key requirement for cruising in the Florida Keys and Bahamian waters.)

BY THE NUMBERS

Ballast/Displacement Ratio 38%
Displacement/ Waterline Length Ratio 347.22
Sail Area/Displacement Ratio (sloop/ketch) 12.19/13.45
Capsize Screening Ratio 1.68
Motion Comfort Ratio 38.3

THINGS TO CHECK OUT

As with any boat two decades old or older, there'll be all sorts of things, both big and small, that will need attention. However, the following items are the most widely recognized:

Despite the fact that the boat has ten opening portlights and three opening hatches, poor ventilation is the most often-heard complaint. This can only be improved upon by the addition of fans, vents, wind scoops, and cruising in cooler climates. Speaking of hatches, over time the Vetus hatches begin to leak and are good candidates for replacement.

There have been numerous reports of significant osmotic blistering of the hull and gelcoat crazing above the waterline. Proper bottom prep and epoxy coating can reduce and even eliminate the blistering, though a new gelcoating or paint job are the only ways to deal with the crazing.

In many instances, owners have replaced the side-loading refrigerator with a top-loading icebox. Side-loaders are notoriously inefficient.

OWNER'S COMMENTS

"...super liveaboard boat, ours has the 'A' interior, it's amazing how much stuff you can store there...we have the ketch version...I wish it pointed higher, but the shoal draft is great in the islands...been living aboard for 4 years..." John N., 1979 model

SUMMING IT UP

The Endeavour 37 is heavily built, with a roomy and nicely finished interior. Its rig is simple and makes for easy and comfortable cruising. Its performance, especially to weather, is lackluster. Plan A is designed for the cruising couple. Its shoal draft won't keep you from gunkholing, nor will it prevent you from venturing into open water. The Endeavour 37 has made safe ocean passages. With 476 boats having been produced, there are always several available. Expect to pay between $34,000 for an early model to $60,000 for a newer boat.

"Only two sailors, in my experience, never ran aground. One never left port, and the other was an atrocious liar."

Don Bramford

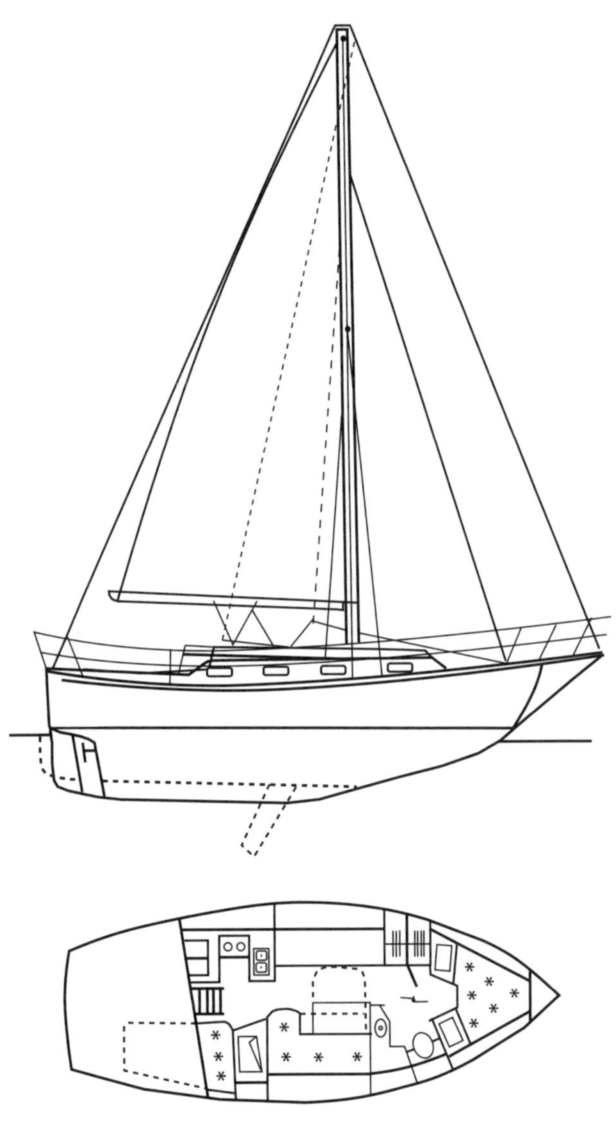

Island Packet 31

Island Packet 31

Not the fastest, but very capable.

Ever since he was a young boy, Robert K. Johnson, founder of Island Packet Yachts of Largo, Florida, had a keen desire to have a career in naval architecture and marine engineering. His first involvement in the field came in 1957, when he was in the ninth grade. Having purchased plans for a 12-foot catboat from *Rudder* magazine, he went about altering the rig and even modified the shape of the hull while he was still building the boat. The project was a success and further fueled his interest in sailboat design.

Having achieved his bachelor's degree in mechanical engineering from the University of Florida, Bob enrolled in MIT, where he obtained his master's degree in naval architecture and marine engineering. Bob's early employment years found him in California, working first in the aerospace industry and finally with Hoyle Schweitzer, who both popularized sailboards and registered the name Windsurfer.

In 1974, wanting to return to both family and boating, Bob went to work for Irwin Yachts in Clearwater, Florida. Here he spent time modifying existing designs, including hulls, rig, keels, and rudders. After about three years, he left Ted Irwin for Endeavour Yachts, an offshoot of Irwin Yachts. It was here that Bob could design boats with his own name on them. He designed the Endeavour 43 and the 40 and 42, both of *Miami Vice* TV fame. This notoriety propelled Endeavour Yachts to become a strong competitor, especially of Irwin Yachts.

Wanting to be on his own, Bob hung out his shingle in 1979, under the name Traditional Watercraft, Inc. His early commissions were small jobs for such companies as Watkins Yachts, CompPac, and Caribbean Sailing Yachts (CSY). Working in his carport, Bob made the molds for the Lightfoot 21, a 1976 design that he had based on a New Haven sharpie. Even though the boat was a bit unusual, he sold eighteen of them. Next, using a set of molds purchased from Bombay Yachts, in 1980 he introduced the Island Packet 26. Later redesigns and modifications resulted in the 26 MK II and the MK III, which was released as the Island Packet 27.

In 1983, Bob bet everything on a completely new boat, one he had designed from the ground up, the Island Packet 31. Introducing the craft that fall at the U.S. Sailboat Show at Annapolis, Bob walked away with orders for 14 boats. Production for the Island Packet 31 continued until 1989, when it was replaced by the Island Packet 32. A total of 262 hulls had been produced during its seven-year production run, more than any other Island Packet design. The gamble had paid off.

Design and Construction

Based on the Island Packet 26, the parent design for the entire Island Packet line, the Island Packet 31 continues the catboat-like look. It features a sweeping sheer, short overhangs including a stubby bow and a nearly vertical transom, and a considerable beam. The cabin top is parallel to the waterline and carries the lines of the yacht out to the stemhead. The boat's maximum beam, carried forward of amidships, forms a "cod's head" contour. This style was popular in the late 19th and early 20th centuries, but is not common among today's modern designs. The hull is U-shaped and, instead of a fin keel, features a long, traditional underbody with a cutaway forefoot. According to Bob Johnson, this is not the full keel of bygone years but rather a modern full-foiled keel. Completing the underwater view is the keel-attached rudder, whose trailing edge is in line with the boat's almost vertical stern. The semi-balanced rudder is comprised of a high-density foam core covered with several layers of fiberglass. The rudder post, of 1½ -inch stainless steel, is driven by rack and pinion steering. A stainless steel heel both supports the rudder and prevents any loose lines from riding up into the propeller. The centerboard, if so equipped, is built similar to the rudder, but is tipped with lead to help keep the board down.

Each Island Packet 31 is fabricated from four major fiberglass components: the hull, the deck, the pan, and the overhead liner. The latter two items are bonded to the hull and deck respectively and make up the yacht's interior.

The hull is a solid hand-laid laminate comprised of multiple layers of triaxial knitted cloth and polyester resin, with an outer skin of conventional fiberglass mat that is covered by gelcoat with an optimum thickness of 25 mils.

The deck is also a hand-laid fiberglass laminate. However, instead of end-grain balsa or marine plywood as the coring material, the deck is cored with ½ inch- to ¾ inch-thick layer of Polycore, Island Packet's proprietary mix of resin and microballoons. The result is an extremely strong composite that is impervious to water intrusion, rot, and delamination.

Being a full-keel design, the hull molding includes a keel cavity. This cavity is filled with ballast bonded in place with resin. Earlier models used lead ingots for ballast, while later versions employed cast iron and concrete. The cavity is then covered with three layers of triaxial fiberglass, effectively encapsulating the ballast as well as creating a second bottom.

After the deck and hull liners are fitted and bonded to the deck and hull respectively, the two assemblies are mated, with a waterproof gasket situated in between. The components are chemically bonded with urethane adhesive and mechanically fastened with ¼ -inch stainless steel bolts on 6-inch centers.

ON DECK

The foredeck of the Island Packet 31 is nearly perfect. The large bow platform, which is surrounded by a stout stainless steel pulpit, extends the boat's LOA to 34 feet 4 inches and easily incorporates two anchor rollers. The toerails are akin to mini bulwarks, and along with dual lifelines, full-length cabin-top handrails and a molded-in antiskid deck make maneuvering on deck comfortable. Add to this wide sidedecks and outboard shrouds.

The uncluttered, expansive cabin top makes for a good work platform. On top, there are three opening hatches (forward, aft of the mast, and starboard over the quarter berth). A fourth hatch over the head was optional. There's also a proper sea hood protecting the companionway, which is offset slightly to port. The cabin trunk features as few as six and as many as eight opening portlights, with the difference being fixed.

The cockpit is comfortable and well designed for cruising. The coamings and bridge deck are easy to step over to reach the deck or to go below respectively. Two large scuppers help keep the cockpit dry. There is a pair of cockpit lockers—a cavernous one to port and a smaller one on the starboard side. The newer models incorporate a centerline swim ladder in the stern pulpit and also offer a cockpit shower.

The deck hardware is above average. Teak is used on the helmsman's seat and ladder rungs, to cap the coamings and toerail, and as trim and accent pieces. Steering is wheel.

BELOW DECK

The layout of the Island Packet 31 is traditional. However, what makes the boat so unique is that all these accommodations and all this livability are packed into just 31 feet. The combination of a relatively long waterline, a wide waterline beam that's carried well forward, and deep bilges results in an immense interior.

Forward, just aft of the divided chain locker with its twin deck pipes, is the 6-foot 6-inch V-berth followed aft to port by a pair of cedar-lined hanging lockers and to starboard by a generous head compartment. The compartment contains a single stainless steel sink with hot and cold pressurized water, a Par head, and a handheld shower that drains to the bilge. There are several lockers and shelves for stowage, plus a convenient dressing seat that folds down over the head. Light and ventilation are provided by an opening portlight and possibly an optional overhead hatch. A folding door gives the forward cabin privacy, while another pair of doors allows access to the head compartment from both the forward cabin and the main saloon.

There are opposing settees in the main saloon. The port settee makes a good single berth, while the starboard L-shaped settee converts to a pullout double. Mounted on the starboard forward bulkhead is a large drop-leaf table, behind which is a spirits locker and shelving for mugs, cups, and glassware. Outboard and above each settee is a full-length fiddled shelf. Six opening portlights, an overhead hatch, and numerous electrical fixtures, one situated between each pair of portlights, provide lighting for the main saloon.

The U-shaped galley, situated to port, features a dual stainless steel sink with both pressurized water and a manual freshwater pump. A stove with oven is outboard, while across from the aft bulkhead is a well-insulated 11-cubic-foot icebox. Island Packet is known for its clever stowage ideas, and this boat abounds with them. There are plenty of nooks and crannies to stow a cruising couples' provisions and galleyware.

To port is a clever arrangement for the double quarter berth and navigation station. By flipping up the chart table and extending a folding pocket door, you can quickly convert the area to a private quarter berth cabin.

The Island Packet's interior is mostly teak, the sole is teak and holly, and headroom is a generous 6 feet 3 inches. Workmanship is excellent throughout.

All tankage, including fresh water, holding, and fuel, is installed just above the keel.

SPECIFICATIONS

LOA	34'4"
LOD	30'7"
LWL	27'9"
Beam	11'6"
Draft	(keel/cb) 4'/3'-7'
Displacement	11,000 lbs.
Ballast	4,500 lbs.
Sail Area	531 sq. ft.

THE RIG

The Island Packet 31 was offered as either a sloop or a cutter (more accurately, a double-headed sloop). Both configurations are low aspect ratio rigs and have the same sail area/displacement ratio of 17.2, which provides adequate performance. Bridge clearance is 43 feet 6 inches. The keel-stepped Isomat spars are anodized aluminum extrusions with internal sailtracks. The standing rigging consists of a headstay, optional inner stay, a pair of cap shrouds, dual fore and aft lower shrouds, and two full-length backstays. There are no running backstays if the boat is rigged with dual headsails. The halyards are cleated on the mast and mechanical advantage is obtained via single speed Lewmar #7 winches. If the boat is equipped with a staysail, it may be either a self-tending clubfooted arrangement or loose-footed. The headsail sheets are led aft via a car and track situated on each toerail and terminated at Lewmar two-speed self-tailing winches mounted on the cockpit coamings. The main is sheeted mid-boom and connected to a traveller mounted just forward of the companionway's sliding hatch and attached to a cabin-top-mounted Lewmar #7 winch.

The Island Packet 31 was first powered with a 22 hp Yanmar diesel. From around 1985 on, a 27 hp Yanmar became the standard power plant. First was the 3GM22F and finally the 3GM30F, an optimized version of 3GM22F. Earlier boats equipped with the 22 hp Yanmar are a bit underpowered. Engine access, rated good to very good, is from behind the companionway stairs and via a large hatch in the cockpit sole.

UNDER WAY

Even though the Island Packet 31's displacement/waterline length and sail area/displacement ratios are similar to those of many production racer/cruisers of the era, the Island Packet 31 was built for comfort and not speed. It is a cruising sailboat, albeit not a heavy one.

The boat's best point of sail is on a reach. Upwind the boat is slow and not very close-winded. The centerboard version performs slightly better on the wind than the fixed keel version. Downwind performance is hampered by the boat's considerable wetted surface. Being full-keeled, the Island Packet 31 is slow to turn. The boat's generous forward beam exacerbates this condition. However, the boat balances well and can steer itself for miles with little attention to the helm, a point in its favor since directional stability is an important consideration when selecting a cruiser. The boat seems to perform well in heavy air. Reefing the main is not necessary until the wind approaches 20 knots. In light air, the boat's performance is lackluster.

About 10 percent of the Island Packet 31s were rigged as sloops while the other 90 percent were double-headed sloops. A sloop with a 150 percent genoa is more efficient, but having two headsails offers the cruiser easier trimming of smaller sails and more sail combinations.

Going forward under power, performance is good. Going in reverse is another story. As with all full keel boats with a propeller in an aperture, backing up can be trying. Also, the three-bladed propeller adds drag when under sail.

BY THE NUMBERS

Ballast/Displacement Ratio 41%
Displacement/Waterline Length 229.8
Sail Area/Displacement Ratio 17.18
Capsize Screening Ratio 2.07
Motion Comfort Ratio 22.81

THINGS TO CHECK OUT

Aside from age-related issues, complaints about the Island Packet 31 are few. Because it's difficult to adjust/replace the packing gland, check this area carefully. Problems can range from excessive water leakage to a scored propeller shaft. The icebox and shower drain into the bilge, which may cause an odor problem. Lastly, there have been some reports of osmotic blistering.

OWNERS' COMMENTS

"...Easily singlehanded. After 12 years, I still enjoy my time aboard. They will have to carry me off..." Jon B., 1986 model

"...It provides all the features that Island Packet is known for and yet on the used market is priced significantly lower than its siblings. The only real challenge for the new 31 owner is learning to back up and this skill can only be learned through practice..." Lawrence S., 1986 model

"...Often after raising sail I just set the auto pilot and sit back, relax, and don't touch a thing until it is time to come about..." Jim E., 1987 model

SUMMING IT UP

The Island Packet 31 is a marriage between a well thought out design and solid construction. It is a spacious, yet relatively small cruising boat, with no pretense of being a performance craft. While the motion comfort and capsize screening ratios suggest that the Island Packet 31 is a fine coastal cruiser, this doesn't mean that it can't safely perform offshore. With proper precautions and good seamanship, the boat will do so quite well.

Since its introduction, the Island Packet 31 has established itself as a cruising classic. And even after all these years, the boat is well supported by its manufacturer. This doesn't come without a price tag. Expect to pay between $44,000 to $65,000.

"Out of sight of land the sailor feels safe.
It is the beach that worries him."

Charles G. Davis

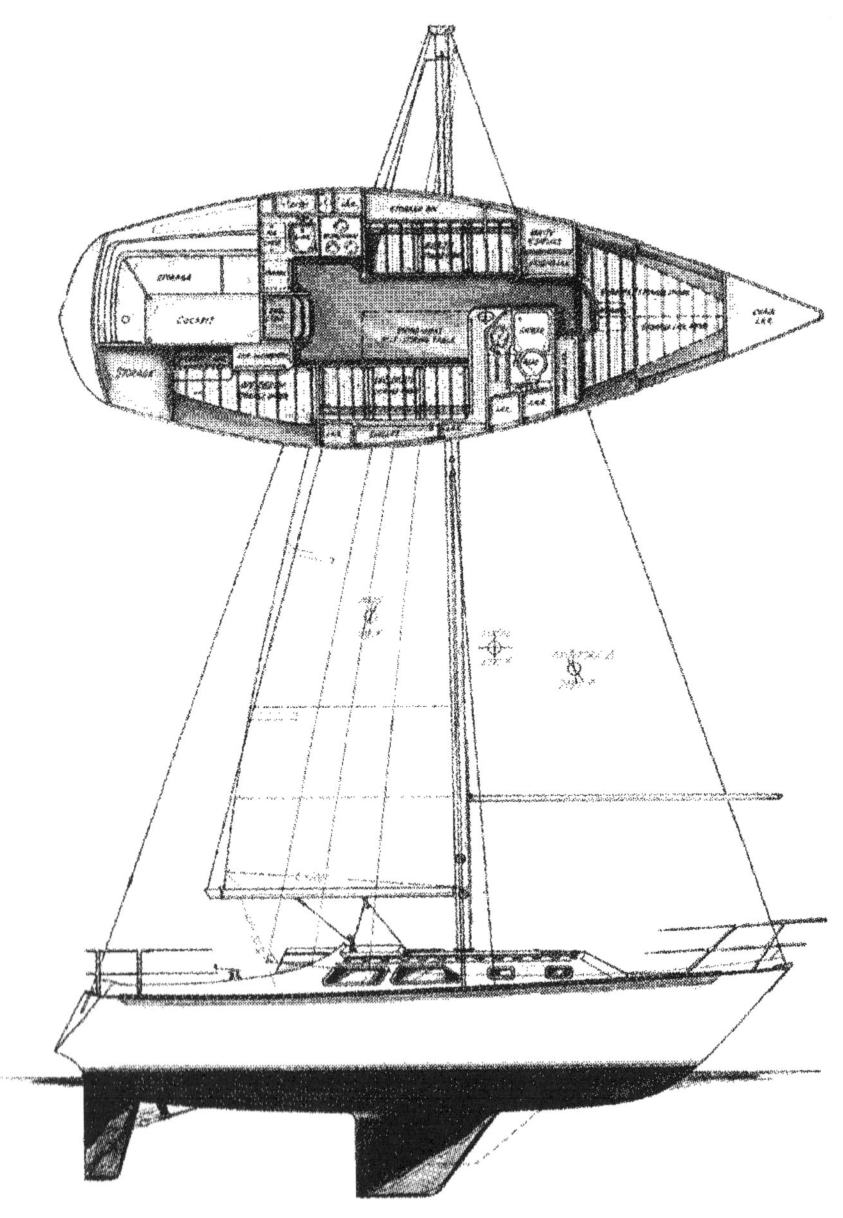

Islander 32 MK II

ISLANDER 32 MK II

Good looking, well designed, and comfortable.

In the mid-1950s, Joseph McGlasson designed and built a 24-foot wooden sailboat that he named the Catalina Islander. The boat, commonly referred to as the Islander 24, was well received and sales were strong. However, like many boat manufacturers of that era, McGlasson recognized the need to switch from wood construction to fiberglass. In 1961 he approached Glas Laminates to help him make that switch and produce his 24-footer in fiberglass. Using a wooden Islander 24 as a plug, a mold was made that carried the original planking lines. These lines became a signature feature of the new fiberglass Islander 24.

While several boats were successfully manufactured, the relationship between Glas Laminates and McGlasson Boat Company was rocky from the start. A less than amicable breakup occurred in 1962, with Glas Laminates and McGlasson Boat Company going their separate ways.

After the breakup, Glas Laminates changed its name to Columbia Yachts and introduced the Columbia 24. Along with the Columbia Challenger 24 and the Columbia Contender 24, the Columbia 24 was curiously identical to the Islander 24, except for the absence of the hull planking lines.

McGlasson Boat Company also stayed busy after the partnership dissolved. By 1963, Joseph McGlasson had incorporated and the new company was renamed Wayfarer Marine. It wasn't until around 1967 that the name Islander Yachts, with the white "swoosh" sail in a black rectangle for a logo, became prominent. Whether Islander Yachts was a subsidiary of Wayfarer Marine or the company's brand name is unclear.

During the next several years, the company was bought and sold several times, with the name Islander Yachts remaining unchanged. In addition to individual owners, Mission Marine, Cosmodyne, Inc., and Radlon, Inc. were a few key corporate owners. In spite of numerous ownership changes and economic downturns, Islander Yachts produced a variety of sailboats from designs penned by several of North America's noted naval architects, including Ted Brewer, Alan Gurney, and Bob Perry.

As a cost-cutting move, Islander Yachts relocated production to Costa Rica in 1984. It didn't help. Two years later—on May 28, 1986, to be exact—the corporation went into bankruptcy, never to build another Islander sailboat.

While Islander Yachts may no longer be in existence, their floating legacy lives on. Islander sailboats ranging from 21 feet to 55 feet can be found bobbing up and down in marinas all over the country.

DESIGN AND CONSTRUCTION

In 1976, the Bob Perry designed Islander 32 MK II was introduced. During its four-year production run, around 200 MK IIs were produced.

With a finely raked bow and a reverse transom, the hull exhibits relatively short overhangs. To please the eye, there is a subtle sheer and a cabin that carries its lines and that of its portlights harmoniously out to the stemhead. The maximum beam is well aft and there is a good amount of flare to the topsides. These last two design elements work together to insure light displacement and a low wetted surface. The reverse transom is wider than the normal IOR (International Offshore Rule) style transom, which was popular at that time. In doing so, Perry created a more comfortable cockpit and added power and reserve stability.

Underwater, the leading edge of the deep (5 feet 4 inches) fin keel is raked aft. In addition to the deep keel version, the boat was also offered with the option of a 4-foot shoal draft keel. On both versions, the rudder, a semibalanced type, is faired into a partial skeg. This arrangement imparts better tracking qualities.

The construction of the Islander 32 MK II is typical of that period. The hull is a solid hand-laid fiberglass and polyester resin laminate. To add stiffness and compression strength, the deck is cored with marine grade plywood. This sandwiching is especially beneficial for all walking surfaces including the cabin top, side decks, and cockpit sole. The hull-to-deck joint appears to be an inward-facing flange that is chemically bonded and mechanically fastened, incorporating a slotted aluminum toe rail.

Rather than a fiberglass pan that's bonded in place, the interior of the Islander 32 MK II is mostly wood and is built into the boat. The bulkheads are marine grade plywood that have been veneered with teak and are tabbed to the hull. Exposed portions of the hull are covered with a padded vinyl liner. Overhead is a zippered vinyl headliner backed with foam insulation. The zippers are strategically located to afford access to through-bolted deck hardware and electrical wiring.

ON DECK

Forward, the stemhead fitting incorporates a single anchor roller; an external anchor locker adequately houses sufficient rode. The deck cleats, on the light side, are good candidates for upgrading. All horizontal surfaces, including the side decks, are molded-in nonskid. However, depending upon age and use, these surfaces may be well worn. The shrouds are mounted inboard, thus improving sheeting angles.

Forward on the cabin top is a large smoked hatch, with a smaller version situated just aft of the mast. There is a sea hood protecting the main companionway, and a pair of long teak handrails. The cabin trunk features a pair of opening portlights forward on each side. Aft of the opening portlights are two much larger fixed ones on each side.

The cockpit is spacious, comfortable, and can be a concern for offshore sailing. Coamings are high, straight, and provide good back support, as well as a place for a pair of cubbies. While there is a pair of cockpit scuppers to drain a water-filled cockpit, the companionway is generously wide and without a bridge deck. Consideration should be given to enlarging the drains or adding additional ones. Also, when sailing offshore or in heavy seas it would be very prudent to keep the lower hatch board firmly secured in place. Located aft are port and starboard cockpit lockers. The latches for these as well as the one for the anchor locker are inadequate and should be upgraded along with the previously mentioned undersized deck hardware. The engine control panel is inconveniently located on the aft side of the footwell beneath the helmsman's seat.

Wheel steering is most common. However, tiller steering was offered as an option. Stainless steel bow and stern pulpits are connected by dual lifelines.

BELOW DECK

Like the Islander 32 MK II's cockpit, the boat's interior is spacious and comfortable, offering considerable stowage for the cruising couple. The finish is all teak, the workmanship above average. Since the interior is built into the boat, the structural integrity and space utilization is considerably better than that of similar sized boats incorporating a fiberglass pan. On the down side, all that wood does make it a bit dark. Fortunately, the large fixed portlights and small overhead hatch help to brighten things in the main saloon.

The layout of the accommodations is quite typical. Forward is the V-berth, which makes for a good-sized double. Outboard are a pair of forward overhead lockers plus port and starboard shelves. Beneath the V-berth is a series of drawers and a couple of bin-type lockers. The large forward hatch and a pair of opening portlights service this area.

Aft and to port is a double-door hanging locker, bureau, and shelf combination. Directly across is the head compartment featuring a stainless steel wash basin; a shower with pressurized hot and cold water; the head; and numerous lockers, drawers, and stowage compartments. Illumination and ventilation are provided by an opening portlight. And privacy is obtained by using the compartment's solid teak door.

The main saloon features offset port and starboard settee/berths and a very large table mounted to the starboard bulkhead. When not in use, the table folds in half, swings down, and is slid between the bulkhead and forward edge of the starboard settee/berth. With the table stowed, the Islander 32 MKII gives the illusion of being a bigger boat than she really is. Above the settee/berths are deceptively large lockers and shelving. Like all the lockers throughout the boat, the doors are faced with natural cane. This is not only an attractive decorative feature, but also allows for excellent airflow.

The L-shaped galley is situated aft of the port settee/berth and consists of a three-burner stove, a single sink with pressurized hot and cold water, and a large top-loading icebox. There's more than adequate counter space for food preparation and enough drawers and lockers to easily handle a cruising couple's galleyware and provisions.

Opposite the galley on the starboard side is a single quarter berth, with stowage below. All berths are a minimum of 6 feet 4 inches in length. There are no provisions for a chart table; any chart work will have to be done on the main saloon's table.

The sole is carpeted throughout, while the headliner is zippered vinyl with foam behind. The zippers allow excellent access to all through-bolted deck fittings and much of the wiring. Where not covered with wood, the hull is lined with off-white vinyl backed with foam. This brightens things up, adds insulation, and is soft to the touch.

Specifications

LOA .... 31'11½"
LWL .... 25'
Beam .... 11'1"
Draft .... (deep/shoal) 5'4"/4'
Displacement .... 10,500 lbs.
Ballast .... 4,200 lbs.
Sail Area .... 523 sq. ft.

The Rig

The Islander 32 MK II is a masthead sloop with a sail area of 523 square feet. The rig incorporates single spreaders and has a bridge clearance of 47 feet from the waterline to the top of the keel-stepped mast. Both spars are aluminum extrusions with internal sail tracks. The standing rigging consists of a headstay, a single pair of cap shrouds, dual lower shrouds, and a split backstay. However, a few boats came from the factory with full double backstays. The halyards are cleated on the mast and mechanical advantage is achieved via a pair of Merriman #16 winches. Although many boats were equipped with end-boom sheeting that led aft of the helm, the Islander 32 MK II was one of the first boats to offer mid-boom sheeting with a traveller situated over the companionway as an option. On each side deck, just aft of the chain plates, a headsail track leads the sheets to a pair of Merriman #20 primaries located midway on the cockpit coamings.

Several different engines were used during the boat's four-year production run. These include the ubiquitous 30 hp Atomic 4, a single cylinder 7 hp Volvo, a twin cylinder 13 hp Volvo, and the 25 hp Westerbeke L25. In every case, fuel capacity is 30 gallons.

UNDER WAY

The Islander 32 MK II is a very nimble sailing boat. It points quite high and balances well. The boat is a bit sluggish in light air, but can stand up to a blow. This is no surprise, since the boat has a displacement/waterline length ratio of 300. At about 20 knots, a reef in the main is required; this will balance out the boat nicely. The helm is responsive and the boat is quick. The boat exhibits practically no weather helm. Although primarily used as a coastal cruiser, several Islander 32 MK IIs have completed impressive offshore passages, including a circumnavigation.

BY THE NUMBERS

Ballast/Displacement Ratio	40%
Displacement/Waterline Length Ratio	300
Sail Area/Displacement Ratio	7.45
Capsize Screening Ratio	2.02
Motion Comfort Ratio	24.16

THINGS TO CHECK OUT

The deck of the Islander 32 MK II is cored with plywood. Sound out the deck, especially around hardware, to determine if water intrusion has taken place.

Osmotic blistering is a common problem with Islander 32 MK IIs. In several cases the problem has been significant. If the bottom looks good, find out what was done (if anything), when it was done, how it was done, and to what extent.

There have been several reports of leaking hull-to-deck joints. Telltale signs include excessive sealant along the toe rail and/or stains on the vinyl hull covering.

The boat has a very shallow bilge; consequently, excess water easily soaks the cabin sole and can damage the lower portions of the wooden settee bases and bulkheads. Speaking of bulkheads, examine carefully where the chain plates are attached to the main bulkhead.

The poor location of the engine control panel lends itself to potential damage. Check it out. Either the Westerbeke L25 or the Atomic 4 is the engine of choice. The small Volvos are just underpowered.

OWNER'S COMMENTS

"...I've owned and lived aboard for 3 years. 1,000 pounds of lead shot was previously added as extra ballast for stability. Construction seems good, but some corners seemed to be cut to save costs. Over all, it is a great boat that sails well to weather and with the added ballast balances very well..."

Victor V., 1976 model

SUMMING IT UP

The Islander 32 MK II is a well designed, strongly built, comfortable cruiser. It is spacious and can easily carry the necessary provisions for a cruising couple. Much of its deck hardware and standing rigging may need to be upgraded for serious offshore work. It sails well and can handle heavy air. The deep draft boat with either the Westerbeke or Atomic 4 is the model of choice; this craft will run $23,000 to $32,000.

"The love that is given to ships
is profoundly different from the love men feel
for every other work of their hands."

Joseph Conrad, *The Mirror of the Sea,* 1906

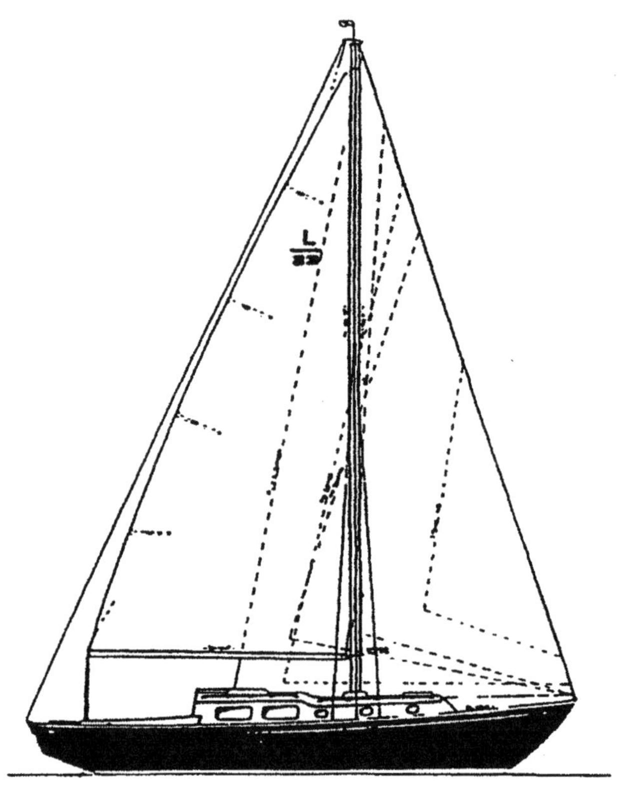

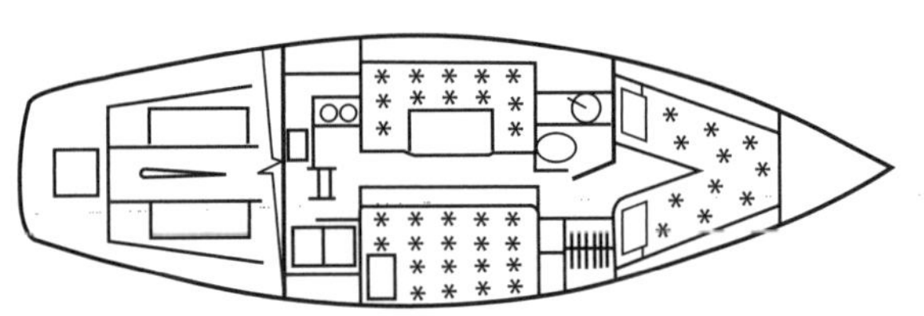

Luders 33

(ALLIED) LUDERS 33

A strong boat and a strong performer with a strong following.

The Luders 33 bears the name of noted yacht designer Alfred Edward "Bill" Luders. Having been a boatbuilder as well as a designer, Bill designed (and his shipyard built) yachts for owners such as King Olaf V of Norway, actor Yul Brynner, Nelson Rockefeller, and the Pulitzer family. Other noteworthy Luders accomplishments include the design of the 1964 America's Cup contender *American Eagle*, the Sea Sprite 34, and a fleet of 44 foot yawls used by the U.S. Naval Academy.

The Luders 33 was one of the most popular and typical of the 1960s racer/cruiser genre. It was designed by Bill and built by the Allied Yacht Company, which was located on the banks of the Hudson River in Catskill, New York. Production of the Luders 33 began in 1966 and ended in 1974. During its production run of nine years, more than 100 boats were built and delivered.

The Luders 33 gained worldwide notoriety as the boat in which Robin Lee Graham became the youngest person ever to complete a circumnavigation. Its heavy construction with design emphasis on seakeeping ability accounts, in part, for the boat's strong following and active owners' association. The boat has a motion comfort ratio of 342 and a capsize screening ratio of 1.71. Both values tend to suggest a comfortable and safe blue-water cruiser.

Design and Construction

From the base of the full keel on up to the gunwale, the hull of the Luders 33 is handlaid, solid fiberglass and polyester resin. As was common for the era, multiple layers of biaxial and woven fiberglass mat were employed. The deck is a fiberglass and balsa wood sandwich. This type of construction creates a strong deck without adding significant weight, provided the outer fiberglass skins are securely attached to the balsa core. Should the bond fail, the three components simply slide over one another as the deck flexes. As a result, structural stiffness is lost. This condition, termed delamination, is worsened by moisture. If the seals around deck-mounted hardware are not vigilantly maintained, water can find its way past the fiberglass skin and into the balsa core. The core then absorbs the water much like a sponge and the grip the resin had on the core is lost. Further, the wet core turns to mush, introducing additional water that can migrate throughout the core, exacerbating the problem.

At the gunwale of the Luder 33, the hull curves inward to create an inboard flange. A corresponding deck flange is rested on this inboard hull flange, sealed with adhesive, and then fastened every 4 inches with bolts and lock nuts. The result is a hull-to-deck joint that finishes flush with the deck. Covering the joint is a teak toe rail.

The full keel is constructed of 4,500 pounds of lead ballast that is encapsulated within the fiberglass keel molding. With a displacement of 12,800 pounds, the Luders 33 has a ballast/displacement ratio of 35 percent.

The rudder is comprised of two fiberglass skins that define its shape, a steel mandrel that is an extension of the rudder post, and a synthetic foam core which both fills the void between and bonds together the two skins and mandrel. The rudder, mounted on the aft edge of the keel using cast bronze gudgeons, has an aperture for the propeller. The rudder post itself is a thick-walled bronze pipe that rides on three Delrin bushings (top, bottom, and cockpit sole).

ON DECK

The foredeck with its two chocks and deck pipe with cover would be exceptional if it weren't for the placement of its single bow cleat, located slightly forward and smack dab in its middle. While the cleat's functionality is good, its potential as a tripping hazard is excellent. The side decks are wide and easily manageable. This is aided by the fact that the shrouds are located outboard and that long, teak handrails are situated on either side of the cabin top. To aid in a secure footing, all horizontal areas are covered in a textured nonskid gelcoat.

Located on the cabin top is the forward hatch. Following this is a pair of Dorade ventilators and finally the main companionway hatch. There is no sea hood. Additional illumination/ventilation is afforded by six opening portlights in the forward portion of the cabin. Four fixed portlights in the raised doghouse area provide illumination only.

The cockpit is short and is surrounded by teak coamings. It contains generous port and starboard seat lockers plus a lazarette. There are four cockpit drains, one located in each of the four corners of the sole. They can adequately drain normal accumulations of rainwater and sea spray. However, should the cockpit get pooped from a following wave, they may be quickly overwhelmed. To exacerbate the condition, there is no bridge deck to keep water from cascading down below. Keeping the lower drop board secured in place will have to do. Lastly, steering is by tiller; however, many boats have been fitted with a wheel.

BELOW DECK

The Luders 33 may seem cramped when compared to the beamy interiors of today's floating condos. However, it is spacious for a boat whose waterline is a mere 24 feet, and it does afford 6 feet 1 inch headroom.

Starting at the stem is a chain locker followed aft by a V-berth. With the addition of an insert, this converts into a comfortable double. There's stowage beneath and on a pair of outboard fiddled shelves. Privacy from the head and main saloon is achieved by closing a pair of wooden doors. Light and ventilation are provided by means of the forward hatch and a pair of opening portlights.

The head with sink and vanity is located to port. There is no shower and the boat originally came with pressurized cold water only. To starboard is a hanging locker and a bureau. A pair of opening portlights as well as a pair of Dorade ventilators service this area.

The main saloon is characterized by a U-shaped dinette to port with stowage beneath and outboard. The dining table can be lowered to convert the dinette into a double berth. To starboard is an upper pilot berth and a lower pull-out transom settee/berth. Abaft the main saloon is an athwartships galley. Situated to port is a two-burner pressurized alcohol stove. The fuel tank for the stove is located beneath the galley stowage locker on the port side. Also to port is a single stainless steel sink with pressurized cold water. The potable water tank is located in the bilge at the foot of the companionway. Additionally, a manual seawater pump can be fitted in the sink's drain. Configured this way, the drain line becomes the seawater supply line. Counter space runs along the aft bulkhead. To starboard is a 12-cubic-foot icebox that drains to the bilge; with its cover closed, it functions as the chart table.

Removing the companionway steps, the cabinet beneath, and a couple of side panels gives almost complete access to the engine. The fuel tank is situated on the centerline and located aft of the engine, beneath the cockpit sole.

The raised doghouse with four large fixed portlights provides headroom, light, and protection for the cockpit. Two opening portlights augment the ventilation provided by the main companionway hatch. Most interior surfaces are plastic laminate with teak joinery, while the sole is teak and holly. The quality of the finish and workmanship is average. While the décor may be somewhat plain, there is no doubt that the basic construction of the Luders 33 is rugged.

SPECIFICATIONS

LOA	33'1"
LWL	24'0"
Beam	10'0"
Draft	5'0"
Displacement	12,800 lbs.
Ballast	4,500 lbs.
Sail Area	574 sq. ft.

THE RIG

The Luders 33's mast is stepped on deck and supported below by a teak compression post fiberglassed to the keel. The mast is an anodized aluminum extrusion with an externally mounted sail track; the boom is also aluminum, while the single pair of spreaders is wooden. The standing rigging is comprised of a forestay, a pair of cap shrouds, fore and aft lowers, and a split backstay. The chain plates are outboard and penetrate the deck, where they are through-bolted to glassed-in wooden knees that are attached to the hull.

Although short, this masthead rig with its big mainsail and small fore triangle provides plenty of power. The Luders 33's sail area/displacement ratio is 16.8. As with several of the Luders' contemporaries, the large mainsail makes the boat easy to handle under mainsail alone.

The halyards are external and are cleated at the mast. To aid in hoisting the sails, a pair of Barient #3 winches is provided. The outboard genoa tracks lead to Barient #22 single speed winches and associated horn cleats situated on fiberglass pedestals located just outside of the cockpit coamings.

The main is sheeted at the boom's end and is attached to a traveler located on the aft deck just forward of the lazarette hatch.

For auxiliary power, the Luders 33 will be equipped with either the original Gray Marine 25 hp engine or, if after 1967, the 27 hp Palmer. Both are gasoline engines; either provides sufficient thrust to push the boat ahead. However, the size and location of the propeller make backing less efficient.

UNDER WAY

Categorized as a very heavy displacement cruiser, with a displacement/length ratio of 413.4, the Luders 33 is hardly a spritely performer, but neither is it a slouch. In the late 1960s, and against its contemporaries, the boat compiled a noteworthy racing record. The boat comes into its own and does best in moderate winds of 15 knots or so. When the wind begins to pick up, it's time to shorten sail to avoid being overpowered. While the boat may heel a bit more than boats with broader beams, the heavy keel will help it to stiffen up quickly.

BY THE NUMBERS

Ballast/Displacement Ratio	35%
Displacement/Waterline Length Ratio	413.36
Sail Area/Displacement Ratio	16.78
Capsize Screening Ratio	1.71
Motion Comfort Ratio	34.23

THINGS TO CHECK OUT

Before you reach for your wallet, remember that a Luders 33 could have celebrated 30 or more birthdays, and a boat that old has experienced its share of both good and bad. For starters, investigate the hull-to-deck joint for leaks, look for damaged bulkhead tabbing, and also check out the rudder and its attachments. Carefully examine the mast step and the compression post, especially below the cabin sole where it meets the keel. Also try to determine the condition of the wooden knees to which the chain plates are attached. Gelcoat problems are common and so is the potential for delamination of the cored deck.

If the boat you're looking at is still powered by a gasoline engine, consider upgrading the power plant with a diesel. Here's where a good surveyor can pay for himself.

OWNER'S COMMENTS

"...the boat is a bit old-fashioned, some would even call it cramped, but with a little imagination and a few modifications it works well for two... we have been living aboard for six years...had to replace the compression post...and upgraded to a diesel..."

Ken H., 1971 model

SUMMING IT UP

The Luders 33 is a very robust, yet sleek sailboat with a full keel, heavy displacement, and low aspect rig. Its design is quite traditional, exhibiting moderate fore and aft overhangs, a modest topside height, and a pleasant sheer. When compared to many of its contemporaries, the Luders 33 sails better than most. Built with strong scantlings, the boat represents good equity. Consequently, refurbishment and upgrading would be worthwhile. Prices for a Luders 33 range from $28,000 to $31,000 depending upon condition.

"The cabin of a small yacht is truly a wonderful thing;
not only will it shelter you from the tempest,
but in the other troubles of life
which may be even more disturbing,
it is a safe retreat."

L. Francis Herreschoff

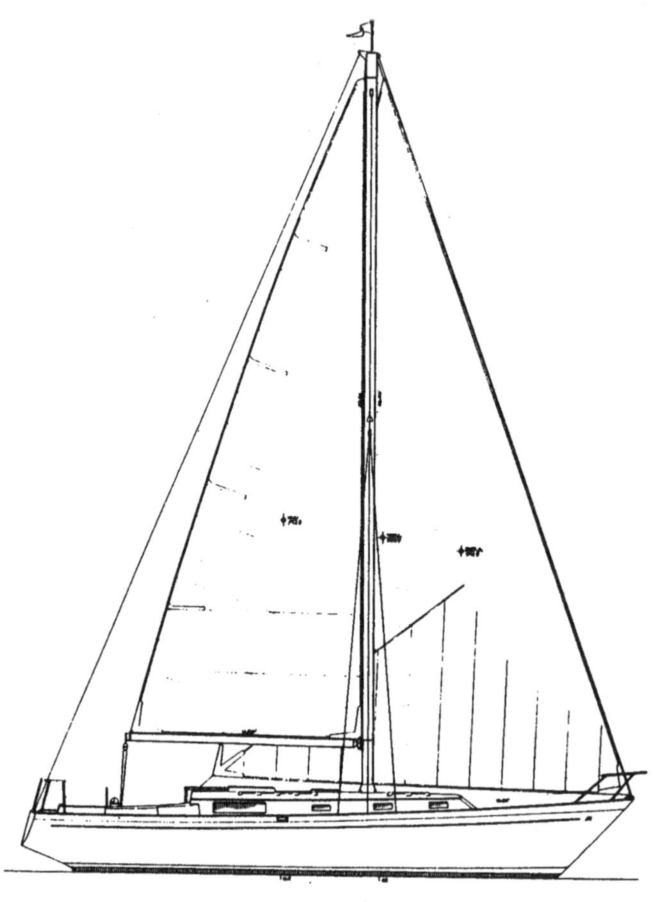

Morgan 382

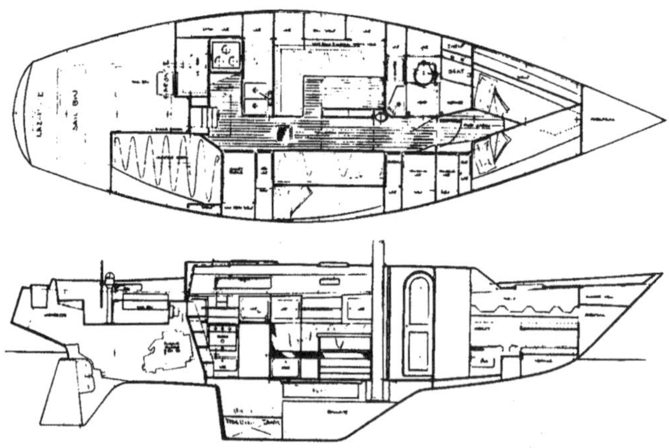

Morgan 382 (383 & 384)

Popular and handsome.

Charley Morgan's obsession for sailboats began at the early age of 10, when his aunt took him sailing on Lake Conway near Orlando. By the time he was 17 years old, he and his sailing buddy, Bruce Bidwell, had successfully competed in the St. Petersburg, Florida to Havana, Cuba sailboat race. This was the first of several sailboat-racing and design accomplishments.

Shortly after graduating from the University of Tampa with a business degree, Charley went to work for Johnson Sails of Tampa as a sailmaker. In 1952, he ventured out on his own and opened Morgan Racing Sails in St. Petersburg. At every opportunity he raced sailboats and, when not racing them, he designed them.

In 1961 he formed Morgan Yacht Corporation, which he located in St. Petersburg. However, a bout with tuberculosis hospitalized him, and his company lay dormant during his illness. Charley *was* the company. Recognizing the need for better business continuity, Charlie tracked down his childhood friend and sailing buddy, Bruce Bidwell.

Under Morgan/Bidwell leadership, Morgan Yacht Corporation delivered its first sailboat in September 1965. Success came quickly, and in December of that year, the company had to temporarily suspend accepting orders because of a huge backlog of orders.

The Morgan 38, designed by Charley, was introduced in 1969. It was a keel-centerboard, CCA-style of yacht. Seventy-nine boats were built before its production ceased in 1971.

Under Ted Brewer and Jack Corey of the Morgan design team, a new Morgan 38 was introduced in 1977. Named the Morgan 382, it was a completely different design featuring a cruising fin keel, a skeg-mounted rudder, a broader beam, and a heavier displacement. After being given a taller rig with a shorter boom in 1980, the boat was renamed the Morgan 383. In 1983, the boat's rudder was enlarged and its interior was slightly modified. The boat was redesignated the Morgan 384. The three Brewer/Corey versions account for 500 boats delivered.

During the production of the Morgan 38, 382, 383, and 384, the company changed ownership several times. It first merged with Beatrice Foods, then was bought by Thor Industries, and in 1983 was finally purchased by Catalina Yachts. Before discontinuing production in 1986, Catalina built 24 Morgan 384s.

DESIGN AND CONSTRUCTION

The design of the Morgan 382 affords roominess and comfort in a very moderate and powerful hull having a displacement/waterline length ratio of 268. The rake of the bow is straight, as is the counter. These moderate overhangs are connected by a gently sweeping sheer and a generous freeboard. Two keel configurations were designed and built. The standard was a 5-foot shoal keel. An optional 6-foot deep keel was also available. Both keel designs have internal lead ballast that has been encapsulated with fiberglass. Completing the underwater design is a full skeg with a large propeller aperture and skeg-mounted rudder.

Most Morgan 382s feature heavy handlaid fiberglass hulls with alternate layers of fiberglass mat and roving and an outer layer of Coremat cloth. While the hulls of the earlier boats were solid fiberglass, many of the later ones were cored with Airex (PVC) foam. Also, prior to 1984, Hetron-brand fire-retardant resin was used in the lamination process. However, it was discontinued after it was blamed for possibly causing blisters. The deck of the Morgan 382 is an Airex-cored fiberglass sandwich that features a molded-in nonskid pattern. The toe rail is actually more of a bulwark and is capped with teak. At its lowest point it is 4 inches high; an inward-turning flange makes this hull-to-deck joint a little costly but significantly stronger.

ON DECK

The foredeck of the Morgan 382 is narrow and is taken up by the large forward hatch. Hardware includes a pair of mooring cleats, a deck pipe, and the stainless steel bow pulpit. The combination of molded-in nonskid, high bulwarks, teak handrail, dual lifelines, and wide side decks makes for easy and safe fore and aft on-deck movement. The cabin top forward of the mast is clutter-free; aft of the mast it features a hatch over the main saloon and a sea hood. There are eight portlights on the cabin trunk: The forward six open, while the aft two are fixed.

The cockpit is roomy, self-bailing, and T-shaped. The coamings are wide and capped with teak. They are also tall and afford good back support. There's a cavernous cockpit seat locker on the port side, another locker beneath the helmsman's seat, and a lazarette abaft the helmsman's hump. There's a teak bridge deck, beneath which is the engine's control panel and above which is a pair of louvered companionway doors. A stainless steel stern pulpit with built-in centerline swim ladder surrounds the cockpit. Steering is wheel.

BELOW DECK

In the forward cabin, the port and starboard sides of the V-berth are tiered. The toe of the port berth extends beneath the toe of the starboard berth. This arrangement is an improvement over a conventional V-berth, especially for tall sailors. There is ample stowage with several drawers, a hanging locker, and overhead bookshelves to port. A louvered door in the forward bulkhead gives access to the chain locker. Privacy for the forward cabin is gained by means of a hinged teak door.

Aft of the forward cabin and on the port side is the head compartment. In addition to the head and a single sink with pressurized hot and cold water, this compartment has an enclosed shower stall with seat. The fiberglass unit is fairly roomy and is designed for easy cleaning. On the starboard side, opposite the head is a large hanging locker and more stowage. In fact, there are over 40 lockers, bins, and drawers throughout the boat.

The main saloon consists of an L-shaped dinette to port and a straight settee/berth to starboard. The centerline drop leaf table is situated just aft of the mast and houses a spirits locker. Above the dinette (which converts into a double berth) are outboard cupboards and shelving. A single pilot berth is situated outboard of the starboard settee/berth.

Aft and to port is the U-shaped galley. There's a single stainless steel sink with pressurized hot and cold water as well as a foot pump for potable water. Other amenities include a two-burner alcohol stove with oven, an 8 ½-cubic foot icebox, and a dedicated garbage bin. There's plenty of stowage for a cruising couple's dry goods and galleyware. Potable water capacity is about 55 gallons.

Across from the galley is the navigation station. The head of the double quarter berth serves as the seat for the good-sized chart table. Lastly, a wet locker is conveniently located by the companionway.

The main saloon features a night lighting system, and there are no fewer than eight teak and brass grabrails. Since the interior sports a lot of wood, it can be on the dark side. While most surfaces are teak veneered plywood, several are white and trimmed in teak. The sole is teak and holly and the ceiling is white with ash battens.

SPECIFICATIONS

LOA .... 38'4"
LWL .... 30'6"
Beam .... 12'
Draft .... (shoal/deep) 5'/6'
Displacement .... 17,000 lbs.
Ballast .... 6,800 lbs.
Sail Area .... 668 sq. ft.

THE RIG

The Morgan 382 is a masthead-rigged sloop incorporating a single pair of spreaders. The boat has a sail area of 668 square feet and a sail area/displacement ratio of 16.49. Its mast is keel-stepped and is 50 feet 6 inches above DWL (54 feet for 383 and 384 versions). Both spars are anodized aluminum extrusions supported by a forestay, single backstay, a pair of cap shrouds, and fore and aft lower shrouds. The shrouds are fastened to chain plates that are located inboard, facilitating better sheeting angles.

Tracks and cars for the headsail sheets are located on the side decks, while the primary winches and cleats are on the cockpit coamings. The mainsail is sheeted end-boom and the mainsheet traveler bisects the cockpit just forward of the helm. A halyard winch is conveniently located on the cabin top.

Two different engines were used as auxiliary power. Early on it was the 33 hp Yanmar 3QM30. This engine was quite noisy and vibrated a great deal. Newer Yanmars have been significantly improved. However, the most common engine is the 50 hp Perkins 4-108. This is the power plant of choice. In both instances they turn a two-bladed propeller and have a fuel tank capacity of 40 gallons.

UNDER WAY

The Morgan 382 is a stable, dry cruiser. It's faster than the original Morgan 38. This is attributable to 382's higher aspect ratio rig, fin keel, and less wetted surface. It points fairly high and performs reasonably well on a reach. It doesn't balance as well as one would like, and when sailing off the wind, it experiences difficulty in tracking, but these pros and cons are all trade-offs and are not unusual. They are directly related to beamy boats with fin keels, which describes the Morgan 382.

Under power the boat maneuvers well going forward. Backing down is another story: one should exercise caution. Access to the engine is average.

BY THE NUMBERS

Ballast/Displacement Ratio	40%
Displacement/Waterline Length Ratio	267.49
Sail Area/Displacement Ratio	16.49
Capsize Screening Ratio	1.87
Motion Comfort Ratio	29.01

THINGS TO CHECK OUT

All in all, the Morgan 382 is a pretty problem-free boat. However, there are a few areas that require a closer look.

Examine the skeg for any possible damage resulting from contact with an underwater obstruction.

On any pre-1984 boat, check the hull for blistering. Generally, some blistering has been reported, but the hulls with Hetron-brand resin may be at greater risk.

Some early boats didn't have the aft bulkhead in the head fiberglassed to the hull. In spite of an aggressive company recall, there may be a boat out there that was not repaired.

OWNERS' COMMENTS

"...excellent windward sailing capabilities...lot of boat for the buck... solid and reliable blue-water boat...I've lived onboard for 4 years...the only weakness noted is the potential for blisters..." Tony C., 1978 model (382)

"...she sails well...we love our boat...we lived aboard for the past year...weakness: fuel tankage is only 40 gallons..." Ed O., 1983 model (384)

"...functional, seaworthy, comfortable...we have lived aboard for a year now...weaknesses are limited tankage, over-all access, some things done by the factory just don't make good sense..." Steve B., 1984 model (384)

SUMMING IT UP

The Morgan 382 and its permutations are strongly built, comfortable, good-looking cruisers. Those that pass a professional survey are capable of transporting the cruising couple and all their necessary gear just about anywhere. Expect to pay around $34,000 to $60,000 for a 382 version. Add maybe another $10,000 for a late model Morgan 384.

"What is more pleasant than a friendly little yacht,
a long stretch of smooth water,
a gentle breeze, the stars?"

William Atkin

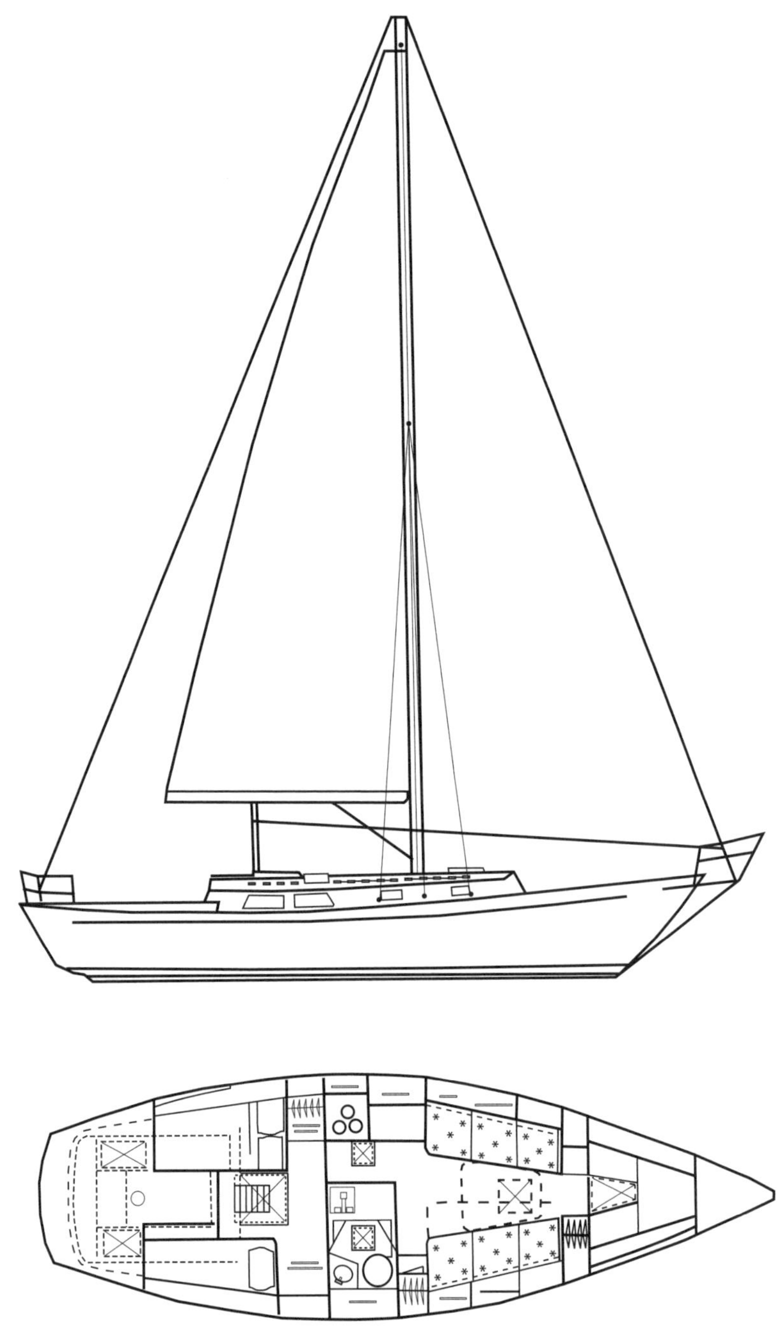

Niagara 35

NIAGARA 35

Close to setting the standard for the ideal cruising boat.

George Hinterhoeller was an Austrian immigrant and a trained boatwright working for a Niagara-on-the-Lake, Ontario yacht builder. It was 1959 and George had a dream. He wanted a sailboat big enough to handle what Lake Ontario could dish out, and it had to be fast.

His dream became a reality in the form of the 24-foot, fin-keeled Shark. Though he had originally produced the boat out of plywood, George responded to customer requests and switched to fiberglass, even though he didn't much care for the material. The Shark was one of the first mass-produced fiberglass sailboats, with 2,500 hulls eventually being made.

In 1969, after his success with the Shark, George became one of the founding fathers of C&C yachts, along with George Cuthbertson, George Cassin, and others. During his tenure with C&C, George helped turn out hundreds of popular, well-built sailboats. Yearning to build boats rather than spend countless hours in the boardroom, George left C&C in 1976.

In 1977 he founded Hinterhoeller Yachts Ltd. and began utilizing the talents of Canadian designer Mark Elllis. Mark was a self-taught designer whose experience had been garnered in the prestigious offices of such noted naval architects as C. Raymond Hunt, Philip L. Rhodes, Ted Hood, and C&C Yachts.

Hinterhoeller Yachts' business plan called for the production of two distinct product lines. At the 1978 Toronto International Boat Show, the Nonsuch 30, with its unstayed mast and wishbone boom, and the more traditional Niagara 35 blue-water cruiser, were introduced.

Approximately half of the 260 Niagara 35s built at Hinterhoeller Yachts' St. Catharines, Ontario plant were destined for the U.S. market. The last hull left the shop in 1990.

George retired in the late 1980s and subsequent changes in ownership and a fire took their toll. The company closed its doors for good in November 1995.

DESIGN AND CONSTRUCTION

Mark Ellis may have come very close to setting the standard for the ideal cruising boat with his design for the Niagara 35. The boat is a thoughtful blend of the traditional and the contemporary. The result is longevity in the way of eye appeal and overall durability.

The Niagara 35 exhibits a pronounced sheer, a straight bow, balanced overhangs, a box-shaped cabin trunk, and high topsides. The underwater profile reveals a cruising fin keel and a balanced spade rudder, without a skeg. The hull is somewhat V-shaped, an IOR design characteristic, which increases the wetted surface but ultimately is more sea-kindly.

Both the hull and deck of the Niagara 35 are fabricated of unidirectional fiberglass roving and resin; hull and deck are cored with balsa. This composite results in a high degree of structural stiffness without adding weight. The balsa core also affords some degree of insulation and soundproofing. While there are several pluses to balsa coring, it is important to make sure that the core material is intact and has not become wet.

All structural members and bulkheads on the Niagara 35 are securely and neatly bonded to the hull with fiberglass cloth and resin. The hull-to-deck joint is chemically bonded and the 5,500 pounds of lead ballast is external and is bolted to a deep and well-reinforced sump.

All deck hardware is of good quality, incorporates backing plates, and is properly reinforced. Below the waterline, the balsa core around through-hulls has been removed and is isolated with resin to minimize water intrusion.

ON DECK

The foredeck is large and features a generous forward hatch, a pair of mooring cleats, a deck pipe, and a tubular stainless steel bowsprit with rod bobstay. The bowsprit incorporates a pair of anchor rollers, which makes for convenient handling and storage of ground tackle. It also functions as the attachment point for the headstay. The stainless steel bow pulpit and dual lifelines give one a good sense of security, as do the 4-inch-high bulwarks.

The side decks are quite wide and, with the shrouds fastened inboard plus conveniently located cabin-top teak handrails, maneuvering about is reasonably secure.

The cabin top is slightly cambered and features two small opening hatches forward, a Dorade ventilator, a pair of larger hatches over the main saloon, and the sea hood. There are eight portlights situated along the cabin trunk. The forward four open, while the slightly larger aft four are fixed.

The cockpit is designed with cruising in mind. It is both comfortable and generously sized. Beneath the port and starboard cockpit seats are lockers, and underneath the helmsman's seat is a propane locker that can conveniently house two 10-pound tanks. Depending upon the boat's interior configuration, the companionway may be either centered or offset to starboard. In either case, the cockpit is self-bailing and features a bridge deck. All deck and cockpit trim is teak. The stainless steel stern pulpit, a pair of aft mooring cleats, and a centerline swim ladder complete the picture.

BELOW DECK

The Niagara 35 demonstrates that there are still more ways to arrange the interior of a small yacht. The boat was originally built without the ubiquitous V-berth. In its place were a workbench, shelves, lockers, and a seat. The main saloon featured opposing settees and a centerline drop leaf table. Situated amidships were the galley to port and the head to starboard.

The main cabin with its double quarter berth was to port and a single quarter berth and navigation station were to starboard. The companionway was centered between the two quarter berths.

This Mk I or Classic version was in production until about 1984. Then, in response to customer demand, the later Niagara 35s were built with a V-berth and a more traditional interior. This version is known as the Encore.

The V-berth of the Encore version features overhead lockers hung outboard and to port, a bookshelf to starboard, several drawers and lockers beneath, and a convenient dressing seat. A hinged door separates the forward cabin from the rest of the boat.

Following aft and to port is the head compartment with its separate shower stall and two doors, one servicing the forward cabin and the other the main saloon. Across from the head is a large hanging locker.

The main saloon with its opposing settees is located amidships. Outboard of both settees are lockers and shelves. A cantilevered, drop leaf table is situated to port; when lowered into position, this converts the port settee into a double berth.

The U-shaped galley is aft and to port and features a gimbaled stove with oven, a dual stainless steel sink with hot and cold pressurized water, an icebox, a generous amount of counter space, and loads of stowage. The companionway is offset to starboard, significantly enlarging the galley.

On the starboard side is the forward-facing navigation station followed aft by a single quarter berth.

The layout of the Encore version is certainly brighter and more open than the Classic arrangement. While some argue that the V-berth is no place to sleep when under way, it is the best place to sleep when at anchor. Also, a V-berth is one of the most efficient ways to utilize the pointy end of the boat.

Both the Classic and Encore versions feature teak bulkheads, doors, and joinery, plus a teak and holly sole. Headroom in both is comfortably in excess of 6 feet.

SPECIFICATIONS

LOA .... 35'1"
LWL .... 26'8"
Beam .... 11'5"
Draft .... 5'2"
Displacement ....14,000 lbs.
Ballast ....5,500 lbs.
Sail Area .... 598 sq. ft.

THE RIG

The Niagara 35 is a sloop with a masthead rig that incorporates a single pair of spreaders. The mast is keel-stepped and the spars are aluminum extrusions. The first five boats were equipped with swaged stainless steel wire standing rigging. Hinterhoeller fit the remainder of the boats with Navtec stainless steel rod rigging. This standing rigging consists of a forestay, a single backstay, a single pair of cap shrouds, and dual fore and aft lower shrouds. There's 598 square feet of sail, with a sail area/displacement ratio of 16.47 indicating a moderately sized rig that should work well in most areas. There are sheeting tracks for the headsail on the bulwarks as well as sheeting leads inboard. The main halyard has its own winch on the mast. Two additional winches are situated aft, on the cabin top, while the primaries are located on the cockpit coamings, within easy reach of the helmsman. Barient winches were initially used and eventually replaced by Lewmar. The main is sheeted mid-boom and, in place of a traveler, two separate tackles are mounted to the cabin top, one to port and another to starboard. The remaining sail controls consist of reefing lines (two reef points are standard), a boom vang, a topping lift, and an internal outhaul.

The original Niagara 35 power plant was the two-cylinder 21 hp Volvo MD11C diesel, which was coupled to a sail drive. In 1982, this unit was replaced by a three-cylinder 27-hp Westerbeke diesel with a V-drive. Later power plants included the Westerbeke 33 and 40 and the Universal M35D. All of these are coupled to a V-drive transmission. Regardless of make, the engine is located below the cockpit. Access for maintenance and inspection is rated as good for the Classic and very good for the Encore. Fuel capacity for both is approximately 30 gallons.

UNDER WAY

The Niagara 35 can be comfortably sailed by a cruising couple. Best of all, most sail controls are close at hand in the cockpit. It isn't a light air boat, but rather favors a bit of a breeze. Under ideal conditions it will easily do 7 knots. Should the wind approach 18 knots or so, it's wise to shorten the sail rather than allow the boat to become overpowered.

The boat points fairly high and sails well to weather. It does OK on a reach. However, on a run it lacks directional stability and tends not to track well. Its high bow allows it to pound through head seas, while its bulwarks keep the cockpit dry.

BY THE NUMBERS

Ballast/Displacement Ratio	39%
Displacement/Waterline Length Ratio	329.47
Sail Area/Displacement Ratio	16.47
Capsize Screening Ratio	1.9
Motion Comfort Ratio	28.71

THINGS TO CHECK OUT

Both the hull and deck of the Niagara 35 are cored with balsa. While this adds strength without adding weight, should water enter the core and saturate it, you will have not only added weight, but also costly delamination.

Have a qualified surveyor carefully go over every inch of the hull and deck, especially around through-hulls and through-bolted deck hardware.

Common problem areas include leaks around portlights and chain plates. Also, there have been a few reports of gelcoat crazing.

Rod rigging has a maximum safe working lifetime. Discuss this with your surveyor and consider possible replacement if the standing rigging is original.

If the boat is equipped with a sail drive, check for corrosion. This is a major problem with saltwater boats. Also, boats equipped with the 21 hp Volvo are underpowered. A better arrangement is a Westerbeke with a V-drive. Speaking of V-drives, the stuffing box is hidden beneath these units and it is hard to service. Check to see that it's adjusted properly.

OWNER'S COMMENTS

"...the perfect boat for a cruising couple...the designer must have known what we needed in a cruising boat...easily handled by the two of us...access to the engine is wonderful, but a little tricky getting to the stuffing box, I made my own tool..." Al & Gerri P., 1986 model

SUMMING IT UP

Mark Ellis seems to have struck a good balance between the requirements for livability and a no-nonsense cruising boat. The Niagara 35 is the kind and size of boat that begins to attract the attention of people who plan to live aboard for extended periods. The two distinctively different interior versions give one a choice. Either is big enough to passage with and provides plenty of volume for a cruising couple's gear and stores.

Prices for a Classic version run between $40,000 and $70,000. Of the 300 or so Niagara 35s built, approximately 75 were Encore versions. These boats tend to sell for considerably more than those with the Classic interior, because the Encore version is more in demand.

"Cruising has two pleasures.
One is to go out into wider waters from a sheltered place.
The other is to go into a sheltered place from wide waters."

Howard Bloomfield

Pacific Seacraft 31

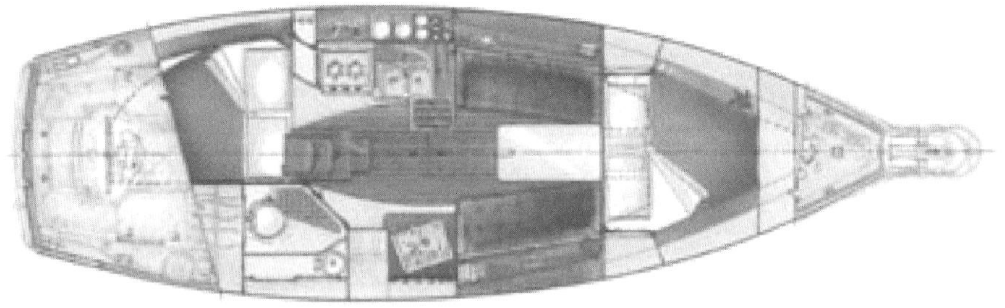

Pacific Seacraft 31

Capable of going a lot farther than you may ever intend.

Pacific Seacraft of Fullerton, California is a well-known, well-respected company that has been producing blue-water sailboats since 1975. The original founders/partners, Mike Howard and Henry Morschaldt, firmly established their company's reputation upon the success of the Flicka, a 20-foot blue-water-capable pocket cruiser. Other notable early offerings included the Orion 27 and Mariah 31.

The year was 1980 when Pacific Seacraft began its association with designer Bill Crealock. In need of something newer and bigger, Pacific Seacraft purchased the molds for the Crealock 37 from a bankrupt company called Cruising Consultants. The design, now known as the Pacific Seacraft 37, is in the Sailboat Hall of Fame.

Born in Essex County in the southwest corner of England, William Ion Belton Crealock began studying naval architecture at Scotland's Glasgow University. Before too long he found a small college in Glasgow that offered evening classes in yacht design. After completing a five-year apprenticeship, he soon found himself spending the better part of his twenties cruising the Atlantic and Pacific oceans.

In 1958, in response to several design requests, Bill opened an office in Newport Beach, California. During those early years, he designed for many West Coast boatbuilders, including Westsail, Ericson, Islander, and Clipper Marine.

After the strong showing of the Crealock 37, Bill designed the 24-foot Dana and the Pacific Seacraft 31. His relationship with Pacific Seacraft began to solidify and, like the company itself, eventually became something very special.

The Pacific Seacraft 31 was introduced in 1987 and remained in production until 1999, during which time 79 hulls were produced. Then, after three years of hearing people request boats smaller than the company was producing, Pacific Seacraft decided that the market justified bringing the 31-foot cutter out of retirement. The boat was reintroduced in 2002 and is currently being manufactured. Thus far, an additional 20 or so hulls have been produced, bringing the total production to around 100 boats.

DESIGN AND CONSTRUCTION

Designer Bill Crealock spent the bulk of his twenties sailing the Atlantic and Pacific Oceans. His designs clearly reflect knowing what works and what is merely eye candy. The Pacific Seacraft 31 is no exception to this. It possesses a lively sheer, a relatively low freeboard, a sleek bow, and, instead of the canoe stern most associated with Bill's work for Pacific Seacraft, a reverse transom stern. The boat exhibits a well-proportioned deckhouse and a traditional wineglass-shaped hull with a long cruising fin keel, bustle, and full skeg-mounted rudder.

The hull of the Pacific Seacraft 31 is solid hand-laminated fiberglass and resin. Next to the gelcoat, the first hull laminate is a layer of chopped strand mat that is wetted out with vinylester resin. This combination affords superior blister resistance. This layer is followed by a mixture of Coremat, fiberglass mat, woven roving, and biaxial roving, each laminated with isophthalic polyester resin. Additional layers are added to high stress areas, such as chain plates, at the rudder post, where the keel attaches, and on the centerline.

While the hull of the Pacific Seacraft 31 is solid fiberglass, the deck is a laminate sandwich featuring a marine plywood core and a molded-in nonskid pattern. The hull-to-deck joint is at the apex of the 4-inch-high bulwarks and is an inward flange that is bonded with polyurethane adhesive and through-bolted with ¼ -inch stainless steel bolts on 4-inch centers. The chain plates are outboard and are through-bolted with ½-inch stainless steel bolts to backing plates and bonded with polyurethane to the hull.

Inside, there's a full-length pan bonded to the hull with fiberglass roving. This component provides structural support and designates foundation areas for the interior features. The partitioning bulkheads are bonded to the hull with fiberglass roving, while the primary structural bulkheads are bonded to both the hull and the deck and are bolted in place.

The keel-to-hull joint is bedded with epoxy and the solid lead ballast casting is fastened to the hull with no fewer than a dozen ¾-inch stainless steel keel bolts. Standard is a 4-foot 11-inch deep keel. An optional shoal-draft Scheel keel that draws an even 4 feet was also available. The ballast, 4,400 pounds of lead, is the same with either keel. The fiberglass rudder features an internal reinforcing steel plate and a 2 3/8-inch stainless steel rudder post. It is mounted to a solid fiberglass skeg, also reinforced with steel, and pivots on a manganese bronze gudgeon.

All deck hardware is of above average quality and is through-bolted and bedded with polyurethane.

ON DECK

At the boat's stem is a stainless steel bow platform that incorporates two bow rollers, locking pins, the attachment point for the headstay, and the bobstay. Except for the staysail's stay, mooring cleats, and a pair of deck pipes leading to a divided chain locker below, the foredeck is roomy. Along with the wide side decks, there's room to move about without negotiating sail tracks or shrouds.

The cabin top is flat and features a large two-way forward hatch, a pair of cowl ventilators with Dorades, four sections of teak handrail, and a sea hood over the companionway sliding hatch. The cabin trunk is literally covered with opening portlights. The four forward ones measure 4 inches by 7 inches, while the aft six are much larger at 7 inches by 12 inches.

The cockpit is slightly T-shaped and features seats that are 7 feet long with contoured backs. Beneath the seats are three lockers. A starboard coaming locker affords vented propane stowage. There's also a contoured helmsman's seat, a pair of safety harness pad eyes, and a broad bridge deck. To aid in keeping the cockpit dry, there are seat drains in addition to a pair of 1½ -inch cockpit drains. While many earlier models of the Pacific Seacraft 31 came with tiller steering, Edson rack-and-pinion steering is standard equipment on the newer boats.

Final touches include a pair of amidships spring cleats, a pair of stern cleats, a stern mounted stainless steel swim ladder with boarding gate, and a stern chain locker with deck pipe and anchor roller. By the way, all deck hardware is chrome-plated bronze.

BELOW DECK

The interior of the Pacific Seacraft 31 provides for amazing openness that may be the envy of many larger vessels. Starting forward and aft of the divided chain locker is a generous V-berth that measures 6 feet 6 inches in length and 78 inches at its widest. For stowage, there are shelves outboard and above, as well as a trio of drawers beneath. A privacy curtain separates this sleeping area from the main saloon.

In the main saloon, a large centerline dining table slides gracefully from its novel stowage area beneath the V-berth to comfortably seat six for meals. Locked into the compression post with a solid 3/8-inch stainless steel pin welded to an internal stainless steel plate, the table takes advantage of the most solid support available. When not in use, the table literally disappears.

The 7-foot-long opposing settees easily convert to sea berths and are equipped with lee cloths. When in use, one needs to sleep with feet forward, since nearly two feet of the berth is tucked beneath the V-berth. When not in use as a berth, this space makes for a good place to stow bedding. There's ample stowage under the settees, as well as in the cedar-lined hanging locker located aft of the navigation station and to starboard.

The galley is aft and to port and conveniently located adjacent to the companionway. There's a remarkable amount of stowage space in lockers, bins, and drawers. Other amenities include a large double stainless steel sink with pressurized hot and cold water, plus manual foot pumps for potable and sea water and a gimbaled stove with oven. The 3.5-cubic-foot icebox is hidden beneath the navigation station on the starboard side, with the chart table doubling as the icebox hatch. Charts can be stowed in a clever tip-out drawer that is sized perfectly for chart books.

The head compartment, located aft of the navigation station, is convenient to the crew on watch. The head compartment offers a wet locker in a proper place—that is, it is easy to reach from the base of the companionway. Other amenities include a vanity, a teak-trimmed mirror, and a sink with a hot and cold pressurized shower attachment.

Opposite the head and beneath the cockpit is a large double quarter berth. This sleeping area can be separated from the main cabin by means of a privacy curtain.

Illumination and ventilation are provided by 10 opening portlights, a pair of cowl vents with Dorade, and the large forward hatch. The interior features a white plastic laminate on the cabin house sides with teak trim, oiled teak bulkheads, a teak and holly sole, and a zippered vinyl headliner that allows access to deck fittings and wiring. Overhead and within easy reach, a pair of teak handrails runs the length of the cabin. Headroom is a comfortable 6 feet 2 inches. There are two potable water tanks, with a total capacity of 65 gallons and a single 23-gallon aluminum tank for fuel.

SPECIFICATIONS

LOA .... 31'10"
LOD .... 30'6"
LWL .... 24'2"
Beam .... 9'10"
Draft ....(shoal/deep) 4'/ 4'11"
Displacement ....11,000 lbs.
Ballast ....4,400 lbs.
Sail Area ....(sloop/cutter) 485/600 sq. ft.

THE RIG

The Pacific Seacraft 31 is offered as a sloop with 485 square feet of sail and a sail area/displacement ratio (SA/D) of 15.7, or as a cutter (actually a double headsail sloop) with 600 square feet of sail and a SA/D of 19.4. In both cases, the mast is stepped on deck and supported below by means of a stainless steel compression post. The standing rigging is 1x19 stainless steel wire and is comprised of a headstay, a pair of single cap shrouds, dual fore and aft lower shrouds, a single backstay, and an adjustable topping lift. Along with the single pair of spreaders, the spars—aluminum extrusions with internal sail tracks—are painted with two-part linear polyurethane. A pair of Harken halyard winches is located on the mast; mast clearance is 44 feet. The tracks and cars for the headsail are situated on the teak-topped bulwarks, while the tracks for the staysail are located on the cabin top. Harken self-tailing primaries along with dedicated cleats are on the cockpit coamings within easy reach of the helm. The main is conveniently sheeted to a traveler on the bridge deck.

UNDER WAY

The long cruising fin keel and skeg-hung rudder contribute to the boat's ability to track well. The boat's best point of sail is a beam or broad reach. Poling out its multiple headsails makes for a stable run downwind. The boat does not particularly shine when going to weather. Less than 40 degrees apparent and the boat's speed noticeably drops. Overall, the boat balances well, is very stable, and is easily handled by a short-handed crew.

The 27 hp Yanmar diesel, which is coupled to a three-blade cruising propeller, easily moves the boat under power. In reverse, the boat tends to "walk" to port. The extent of this walking is determined by the boat's speed. Very good access to the engine is achieved by removing the engine compartment housing. The stuffing box is within easy reach.

BY THE NUMBERS

Ballast/Displacement Ratio 40%
Displacement/Waterline Length Ratio....... 348.22
Sail Area/Displacement Ratio(sloop/cutter) 15:69/19:41
Capsize Screening Ratio..................... 1.77
Motion Comfort Ratio 30.81

THINGS TO CHECK OUT

Pacific Seacrafts have an amazing following. It's almost cult-like in some ways. This is because the boats are purpose-driven, not market-driven. The resultant quality leaves very little room for potential, let alone chronic, problems to occur. Most "problems" that have been reported have been the result of abuse or neglect and, to a lesser extent, age. Have a competent surveyor go over the boat thoroughly.

OWNERS' COMMENTS

"...Excellent joiner work and overall construction. Very easy to handle with a crew of two..." Brad C., 1989 model

"...Outstanding sloop, great to sail, haven't found any weaknesses..." Larry B., 1994 model

SUMMING IT UP

The Pacific Seacraft 31 is designed and built to sail in comfort and confidence. The boat embodies all the Pacific Seacraft trademarks of high quality and attention to detail. For the cruising couple, the boat is easy to handle, surprisingly roomy, and affords phenomenal stowage. Used boats run from about $80,000 to near $100,000. At these prices, one would suspect that the boat would require an absolute minimum of after-purchase expenses.

"Just as beauty in woman creates allure and inspires affection, so it does in a boat."

William Snaith, *On the Winds Way*

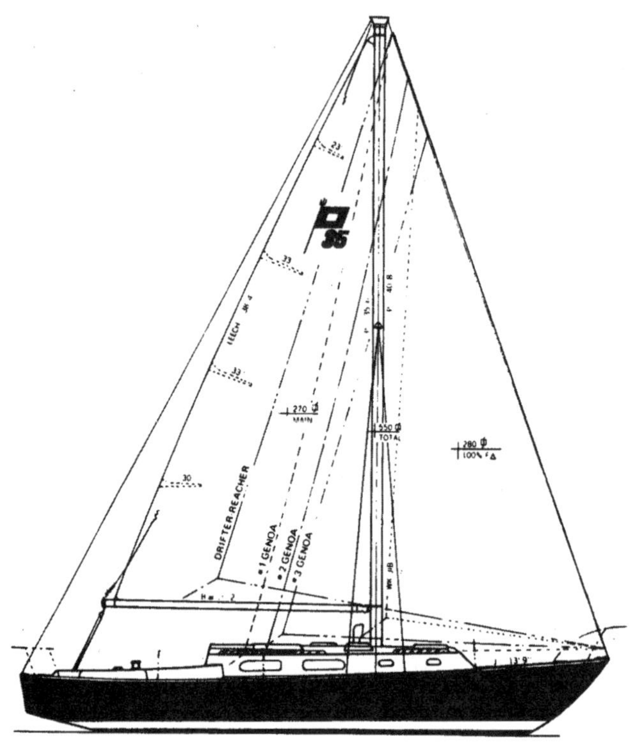
35
LEECH
DRIFTER REACHER
#1 GENOA
#2 GENOA
#3 GENOA
270 MAIN
550 TOTAL
280
100% FΔ

Pearson 35

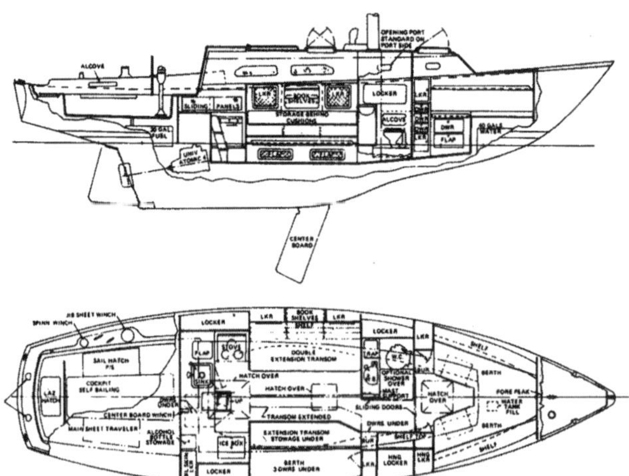
ALCOVE
OPENING PORT STANDARD ON PORT SIDE
LOCKER
CENTER BOARD
JIB SHEET WINCH
SPINN WINCH
SAIL HATCH
COCKPIT SELF BAILING
CENTER BOARD WINCH
MAIN SHEET TRAVELER
STOVE
DOUBLE EXTENSION TRANSOM
HATCH OVER
TRANSOM EXTENDED
ICE BOX
EXTENSION TRANSOM STOWAGE UNDER
BERTH 3 DWRS UNDER
MAST SUPPORT
SLIDING DOORS
SHELF
BERTH
FORE PEAK

Pearson 35

A popular, well-aged, shoal-draft cruiser.

Flush from their early success with the 28-foot Triton, cousins Everett and Clinton Pearson continued to build, almost exclusively, Carl Alberg-designed sailboats. The arrangement between Pearson Yachts and Carl was initially mutually beneficial; however, it soon became lopsided. As part of their agreement, Carl received a royalty on each of his designs that was sold. As the price of the boats went up, so did Carl's royalty payment. In 1964, just a mere five years after the introduction of the Triton, Carl was receiving in excess of $40,000 a year in royalties. Everett tried to renegotiate royalties with Carl, but the "stubborn Swede" refused. This was the end of Carl's association with Pearson Yachts.

A naval architect named William H. Shaw heard about the new opening at Pearson Yachts and went to Bristol, Rhode Island to interview with the Pearson cousins. Bill's experience included 11 years with Sparkman and Stephens and a stint with an outfit called Products of Asia, whose most famous import was to become the Grand Banks line of trawlers. The interview went well and Bill was hired as the director of design and engineering.

That same year, Grumman Allied Industries, who owned the controlling interest in Pearson Yachts, built a new manufacturing facility in Portsmouth, Rhode Island, with plans to move the company there. They also fired Clinton Pearson. 1964 was a memorable year. By 1966, Everett was poised to leave and he did. Soon after, Bill Shaw became the general manager of the Pearson Yacht Division.

Under Bill's leadership, Pearson Yachts flourished. Numerous designs went from his drawing board to the production floor. This included the Pearson 35, which was introduced in 1968 as the direct replacement for the aging Alberg 35.

The Pearson 35 was well received, especially by East Coast and Great Lakes sailors. This was mainly due to its shoal draft, not to mention the boat's classic lines. The Pearson 35 turned out to be one of Pearson Yacht's most successful boats. It was in production for 14 years, a company record. The company never approached that again; most designs would last about five years. When production of the Pearson 35 finally ceased in 1982, 514 hulls had been made. During its production run, the Pearson 35 saw very little in the way of design changes, a testament to its popularity.

Like many other sailboat manufacturers in the late '80s and early '90s, Pearson Yachts was feeling the pressure of an economic recession, the new 10 percent luxury tax, and even competition from their old boats. With sales plummeting, Bill retired just before Pearson filed for bankruptcy in 1991. But with some 20,000 boats out there bearing the Pearson name, the Pearson legacy is well established in the history of boating.

DESIGN AND CONSTRUCTION

Since designer Bill Shaw was partial to centerboarders, it's not surprising that the Shaw-designed Pearson 35 bears the marks of a well-developed CCA (Cruising Club of America) centerboarder. In putting together the Pearson 35, he expertly combined the elements of long yet pleasantly proportioned overhangs, a graceful sheer, modest freeboard, and a not overly long cabin trunk, which made for a very roomy cockpit. The 10-foot beam, narrow by today's standards, dictates a somewhat compact interior. However, the interior is effectively laid out and affords quite an efficient arrangement for a cruising couple. The displacement is quite heavy, revealing a displacement/waterline length ratio of 371. Completing the design is a low aspect ratio main, a modified full keel with centerboard, and a keel-hung rudder.

The Pearson 35 is structurally a rugged boat, and its construction is fairly straightforward. Both hull and deck are handlaid fiberglass laminates. While the hull is a heavy solid laminate, the deck is much lighter and comprised of a sandwich of two fiberglass layers with a core of balsa wood between them. This makes a light and rigid deck. If you recall, Everett Pearson pioneered the use of end-grain balsa as a coring material, and the Pearson 35 benefits from this technology.

The boat's underbody features a 3-foot 9-inch modified full keel with a fiberglass laminate centerboard. The 5,400 pounds of lead ballast is encapsulated within the keel cavity, thus eliminating the concern for loose or corroded keel bolts. The fiberglass rudder is hung from the following edge of the keel and rides on a bronze heel casting.

The Pearson 35's interior is fitted with the combination of a molded fiberglass overhead liner and a pan or hull liner that not only increases the boat's structural integrity, but also designates the location of interior features. The bulkheads and other "furniture" components are plywood veneered with either a wood-grained or off-white plastic laminate.

ON DECK

The sole occupants of the Pearson 35's foredeck are the stainless steel bow pulpit, a pair of mooring cleats, and the hatch to the boat's on-deck anchor locker. This leaves the boat with a spacious forward work platform. The combination of reasonably wide side decks, dual lifelines, a teak-capped toe rail, and four sections of teak handrail aid in secure fore and aft movement.

The cabin top is slightly cambered and features a forward hatch, a pair of cowl vents with Dorades, a second hatch over the main cabin area, and a sea hood. The trunk features four forward opening portlights, two per side, and four much larger aft fixed portlights, again two per side.

The gently sloping coamings frame the boat's strongest appealing feature, its cockpit. Not only is it big, real big (over 9 feet long), but it's also comfortable and efficient. While this amenity is great for entertaining, its size is less than desirable for offshore work. Since the boat does not feature any quarter berths, there are cavernous port and starboard cockpit seat lockers in their stead, plus a usable lazarette and a pair of coaming cubbies. The boat does have a good bridge deck to keep water from cascading below should the cockpit get pooped, but the two small cockpit drains don't appear to be adequate to drain the cockpit quickly.

The Pearson 35 was fitted with wheel steering, with the pedestal being mounted immediately aft of the bridge deck. This not only leaves the balance of the cockpit open and clutter-free, but in case of foul weather, the helmsman can steer from behind a protective dodger. The position of the helm also facilitates easy communication with crew below. One disadvantage is that the helm must be negotiated each and every time a crewmember enters or exits from below. While doing so, especially during bad weather, an unconscious grab of the wheel in search of a handhold could have exciting consequences.

Below Deck

The layout of the Pearson 35's accommodations is very traditional and functional. Starting in the forward cabin, which can be closed off from the rest of the boat with a convenient sliding door, is the roomy V-berth with insert that comfortably sleeps two. For stowage, there are four drawers beneath the V-berth, a chest of three in the port bureau, and two hanging lockers (one cedar-lined) to starboard. The forward overhead hatch and two opening portlights admit light and fresh air.

Following aft and to port is the head compartment. A second sliding door gives this area privacy. Amenities include a single stainless steel sink with vanity, pressurized water, optional shower, a marine toilet, and a pair of lockers. An opening portlight services this compartment. Directly across from the head compartment, on the starboard side, is a large hanging locker plus a pair of drawers situated beneath a convenient counter top, with an opening portlight above.

The main saloon has, to port, a bulkhead-mounted drop leaf table flanked by opposing port and starboard settees. On the starboard side, the settee pulls out and converts to a single berth. Outboard and above is a pilot berth. Starboard-side stowage consists of three drawers and two lockers. The opposing port settee converts into a double (actually a large single), with no fewer than six lockers and a pair of fiddled shelves for stowage. Overhead are an opening hatch and a pair of Dorade ventilators.

Aft of the main saloon, the galley runs athwartships. The pressurized alcohol stove and oven combination are to port. The stainless steel sink, with pressurized water plus manual sea and potable water pumps, is situated on the athwartships counter. And on the starboard side is the icebox, whose top doubles as a chart table. There are numerous stowage opportunities in the form of shelves, bins, and lockers in which to keep a cruising couple's provisions.

Conveniently located on the starboard side and adjacent to the companionway is a proper foul weather gear locker. Four large fixed portlights illuminate the main saloon and galley areas. Those surfaces that are not fiberglass are plywood, veneered with either a white or wood-grained plastic laminate and trimmed with real teak. The sole is the traditional teak and holly; headroom is a comfortable 6 feet 3 inches. Potable water capacity is approximately 80 gallons.

SPECIFICATIONS

LOA	35'
LWL	25'
Beam	10'
Draft	3'9"-7'6"
Displacement	13,000 lbs.
Ballast	5,400 lbs.
Sail Area	550 sq. ft.

THE RIG

The majority of the Pearson 35s are rigged as masthead sloops, with a very few being rigged as yawls. Both the sloop and yawl use the same mast location. It is somewhat forward and therefore results in a small fore triangle and a large, low aspect mainsail. A major benefit of this rig is that the boat can be easily balanced and comfortably sailed under main alone. The sail area of the sloop is 550 square feet, giving the boat a sail area/displacement ratio of 15.92.

The Pearson 35's mast is stepped on deck and is supported below by a weight-bearing bulkhead. A pair of single spreaders, a forestay, single cap shrouds, dual lower shrouds, and a single backstay support the mast. Both the mast and the boom are anodized aluminum extrusions. Bridge clearance is 44 feet 6 inches from design waterline to the top of the masthead.

Both halyards are cleated at the mast, and two mast-mounted winches provide mechanical advantage. The headsail primary winches are mounted on the wide tops of the cockpit coamings. End-boom sheeting controls the main and is attached to a traveler located just forward of the lazarette hatch.

Over the years, the Pearson 35 employed a variety of power plants. First was the 30 hp Atomic 4. This was followed, in the mid-1970s, by the Farymann diesel. The 30 hp Westerbeke replaced the Farymann and the 24 hp Universal replaced the Westerbeke. Some of the later boats are even equipped with 27 hp Yanmars. With 13,000 pounds of displacement to move, all of the engines are modest performers. Moving in reverse can be challenging and takes practice. Fuel capacity is approximately 20 gallons. Access to the engine is poor; it is obtained by removing the companionway steps and a galley cabinet.

UNDER WAY

The Pearson 35 was promoted as a racer/cruiser; however, it is primarily a cruising sailboat. Its displacement/waterline length ratio of 371.4 categorizes it as a very heavy displacement cruiser. This, along with its 10-foot beam, makes for easy motion in a seaway. Its motion comfort ratio is 33.2 and its capsize screening ratio is 1.7. The boat is often referred to as being tender. It does heel quickly, but once it reaches about 30 degrees, it stiffens up. Also, its powerful ends increase the boat's waterline length, and the Pearson 35 struts her stuff.

Overall, the Pearson 35 is a solid performer. While it is a mediocre light air performer, the boat's low aspect ratio main gives it good reaching and running speed. It really shines on a close reach. It's a fast, seaworthy, comfortable, and relatively dry boat. The boat can handle tough conditions without any undo concern; however, the size of the boat's cockpit is a serious consideration for blue-water cruising.

BY THE NUMBERS

Ballast/Displacement Ratio 42%
Displacement/Waterline Length Ratio. 371.43
Sail Area/Displacement Ratio 15.92
Capsize Screening Ratio 1.7
Motion Comfort Ratio 33.18

THINGS TO CHECK OUT

Even though the Pearson 35 is nearly bulletproof, there are a few problem areas that seem to be somewhat chronic. All are age-related.

Over time the deck fittings, including the hatches, portlights, and chain plates, tend to leak, which can cause delamination of the balsa-cored deck. With the mast stepped on deck, check for signs of deck compression and possible damage to the supporting bulkhead.

Unfortunately, a leaking hull-to-deck joint is a common occurrence. A good place to start looking is at any rubrail area that displays the telltale signs of a hard docking.

The centerboard pennant and pivot point are common problem areas; these need to be carefully examined with the boat out of the water.

Lastly, gelcoat crazing is a common cosmetic problem.

OWNERS' COMMENTS

"...front stateroom is considerable and well appreciated by a cruising couple...with a narrow beam and long overhangs, the Pearson 35 behaves extremely well in heavy weather...have sailed our boat in winds over 30 knots and high seas without fear...consider having three reef points, a great asset in heavy winds..." Al L., 1969 model

"...a solid, well designed boat...very comfortable ride in a sea... interior space is very adequate for a couple on an extended cruise..." Tony L., 1976 model

"...strengths are its beauty, its comfort, and its comfortable sailing characteristics...the boat will get you home in any situation..." Louis S., 1980 model

SUMMING IT UP

This is a yacht that combines superb handling, excellent accommodations, and classic lines. The full keel/centerboard configuration provides excellent sailing characteristics in the ocean and the benefits of shoal draft when gunkholing. It is a safe, solid, and comfortable cruiser, with one serious drawback: its large cockpit. On the used boat market, Pearson 35s run from a low of $12,000 for a "needs work" 1968 model to around $40,000 for an '80s version. Before buying an early production boat, consider a newer model. Repowering an older version is challenging.

“It never ceases to lighten my soul when I realize
that through cunning and skill
I have tricked the wind into moving my boat.”

David Seidman

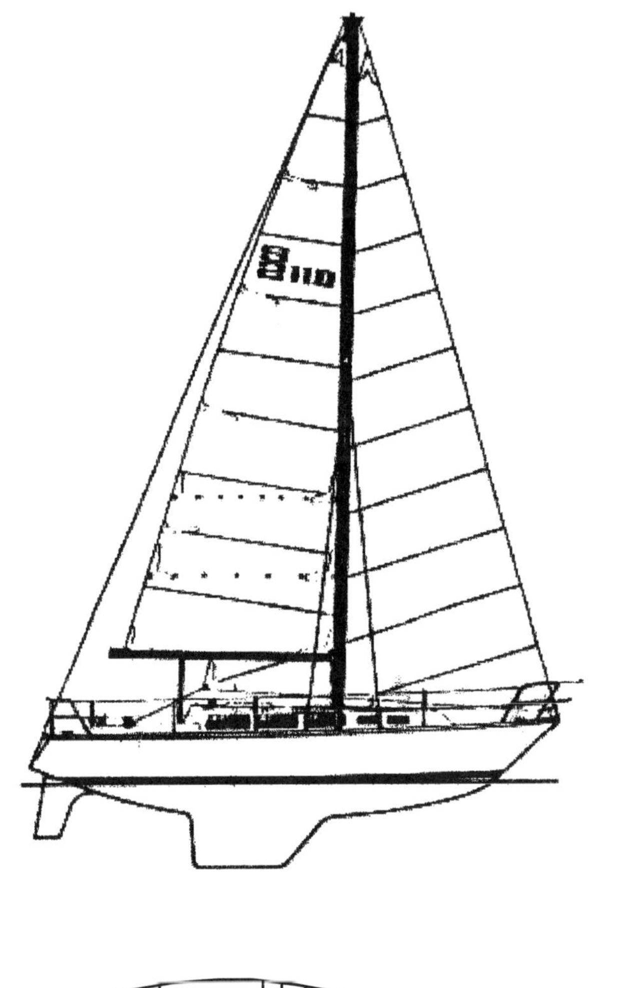

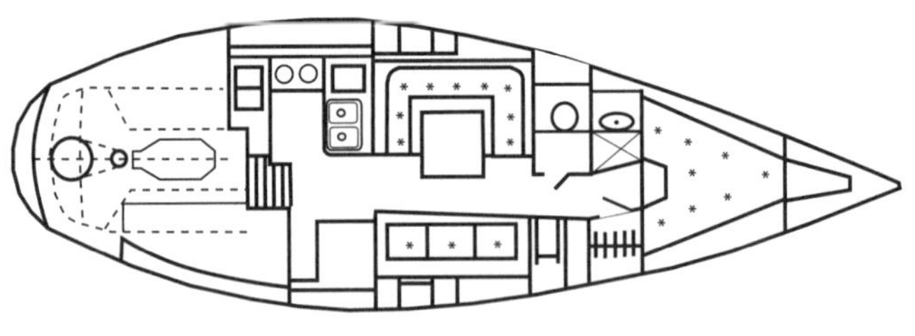

S2 11.0

S2 11.0

A bluewater-capable beauty from the shores of Lake Michigan.

In 1946, 18-year-old Leon R. Slikkers left the family farm in Diamond Springs, Michigan for a job in the joiner department at the Chris Craft Corporation in Holland, Michigan. During his almost ten-year association with Chris Craft, Slikkers refined his skills and was noted for his ability to create new and innovative designs.

During a company-wide labor strike in 1952, Slikkers decided to build boats of his own design. Not unlike many other fledgling boatbuilders, he began production in his garage. While the strike was in progress, he fabricated about ten 15- and 17-foot runabouts out of plywood.

With labor strikes becoming more and more common and his after-hours boat building business becoming more and more successful, Slikkers started thinking seriously about going out on his own. His first step was to register the name SlickCraft in 1954. In 1955, he made his move and during that model year he built 35 boats, all out of wood.

By 1956, Slikkers was experimenting with fiberglass hull construction. He came to understand that fiberglass was the future and switched to all fiberglass construction after the 1962 model year. Innovation and success continued for this small family-oriented company. The SlickCraft name became synonymous with quality and affordability.

After having attracted the attention of a conglomerate, the Slikkers family sold the company to the AMF Corporation in September 1969. Slikkers was retained as president of the SlickCraft Division. His association with AMF lasted four years. Upon leaving, he immediately began experimenting with a fiberglass sailboat design that would not violate his powerboat non-compete clause with AMF.

On February 18, 1974, S2 Yachts, Inc. came into being. While Slikkers's goal was to build a series of well detailed, nicely built, high quality trailerables, his first offerings weren't good-lookers nor did they perform all that well. The joke was that S2 stood for "slowly sideways"! Being a quick study, Slikkers quickly adjusted, and by the late 1970s the company had developed an impressive line of cruising auxiliaries. S2 soon became synonymous with craftsmanship, styling, and performance.

Correctly anticipating the shrinking sailboat market, Slikkers added powerboat production to his product line. This began with the introduction in 1977 of the Pursuit series of fishing boats. Tiara followed in 1979, and in 1983, after purchasing the brand from AMF, SlickCraft sportboats joined the line. S2 sailboat production ceased in 1987.

DESIGN AND CONSTRUCTION

The S2 11.0 was introduced in 1977. Arthur Edmonds of Allied Princess 36 fame designed it. He had also been involved with the Chris Craft sailboat project of the late 1960s. The 11.0, the largest sailboat built by S2, was offered in both aft and center cockpit versions. Approximately 160 hulls of each configuration were sold. The aft cockpit version, the more aesthetically pleasing of the two, is the one that will be featured in this review.

While the earlier Graham and Schlagater-designed Grand Slam series of S2s were high-performance sailboats that had produced a two-time MORC (Midget Ocean Racing Club) champion, the Edmonds-designed 11.0 was all cruiser, and a moderately designed one at that.

To achieve this end, Edmonds combined the design elements of a somewhat flat sheer, fore and aft overhangs, a reverse transom, and a slightly forward-leaning cabin top. In concert these elements produce a balanced and graceful appearance. Unfortunately, the three large aft portlights are somewhat of a distraction.

Underwater there is a cruising fin keel and a low aspect ratio rudder supported by a token skeg. The 6,000 pounds of encapsulated ballast cause the keel to be quite thick, which produces significant drag, and the low aspect ratio rudder negatively impacts the boat's turning efficiency.

The hull is a solid handlaid laminate of fiberglass and vinylester resin. Next to the high quality gelcoat, the first fiberglass layer is chopped mat followed by a succession of cloth layers. The deck is also handlaid fiberglass, with all horizontal areas cored with end-grain balsa. The hull-to-deck joint is an inward-facing flange arrangement bonded with a flexible adhesive and through-bolted on six-inch centers. The resulting toe rail is capped with teak and the actual seam is hidden by a vinyl rubrail.

On Deck

The foredeck on the S2 11.0 is kept relatively dry by the boat's marked forward overhang. While the anchor is secured in a bow roller and the rode is led below through a deck pipe, the two large mooring cleats are positioned outboard on the teak-capped toe rail. This leaves the foredeck, with its two-tone nonskid surface, clear of any obstructions. Security is in the form of a stainless steel bow pulpit and dual lifelines. The side decks are comfortably wide and the shrouds are fastened to chain plates situated inboard.

Forward, on the cabin top, is a flush-mounted, smoked acrylic hatch. This is followed aft by port and starboard cowl ventilators and a second, smaller, flush-mounted smoked acrylic hatch. Both hatches are covered with teak strips to protect them and provide nonskid footing. There's a proper sea hood protecting the companionway sliding hatch and a pair of teak handrails. These port and starboard handrails span the full length of the cabin's top and, since they are recessed, are promoted as being of a nontrip design. While they look great, in actual use they are not easily accessible and are more of a "finger-breaker" design. On each side of the cabin trunk is a forward pair of opening portlights and a series of three very large fixed portlights.

The cockpit is T-shaped and comfortably sized. The wide coamings are of a reasonable height and offer some degree of back support. There's a deep locker beneath the port cockpit seat and a lazarette with access on either side of the helmsman's seat. Wheel steering is standard. There is no bridge deck. A pair of aft cockpit sole drains provides drainage. Dual lifelines connect to the stainless steel stern pulpit, with its integrated centerline swim ladder, which surrounds the aft portion of the cockpit.

BELOW DECK

The forward cabin features a large V-berth with filler, port and starboard outboard shelf stowage above, and a set of drawers and stowage below. To port is a door leading to the head compartment and to starboard a hanging locker, a wet locker, and a suite of drawers. A second door aft leads to the main saloon and affords separation and privacy to both areas.

The port head compartment can also be accessed from the main saloon by means of a second door. The compartment is generously sized and features a single stainless steel sink with vanity, hot and cold pressurized water, a handheld shower, and of course the head. An opening portlight and a cowl vent provide light and ventilation to this area.

In the main saloon there is a single settee/berth to starboard with stowage beneath and behind the cushions. To port is a U-shaped dinette, also with stowage beneath and behind. If one lowers the pedestal table, the dinette converts into a double berth. Outboard and above both settees is additional stowage in the form of cabinets and fiddled shelves.

Aft and to port of the main saloon is the U-shaped galley with a serve-through counter, over which is a ceiling-mounted cabinet with doors on both sides. The galley is workable, spacious, and well designed. It features a dual stainless steel sink with pressurized water, a gimbaled stove, a 9-cubic-foot icebox, and a generous amount of stowage in the form of bins, lockers, shelves, and drawers. Potable water capacity is 80 gallons.

Opposite the galley, on the starboard side, is the forward-facing navigation station. The forward edge of the quarter berth functions as a convenient seat, while the chart table features a hinged foldout portion that, when deployed, creates an even larger charting surface. The entire top also hinges up, revealing stowage for navigational aids below.

Aft of the navigation station is a double quarter berth with full-length stowage cabinetry above.

All bulkheads, cabinetry, and joinery are varnished teak. Locker doors are either louvered or feature natural cane inserts. The overhead is white and battened with teak strips. The sole is teak and holly. The boat's 11-foot 11-inch beam and 6 large fixed portlights create a bright, airy, and spacious cabin with 6 feet 3 inches of headroom throughout.

Specifications

LOA .... 36'
LWL .... 28'3"
Beam .... 11'11"
Draft .... (deep/shoal) 5'6"/4'8"
Displacement .... 15,000 lbs.
Ballast .... 6,000 lbs.
Sail Area .... 632 sq. ft.

The Rig

The S2 11.0 is a sloop with a masthead rig. It features a high aspect ratio sail plan with a small mainsail and an overlarge headsail. The boat's sail area/displacement ratio is a moderate 17.2. The mast is keel-stepped and has a bridge clearance of 49 feet. Both spars are painted aluminum extrusions. A pair of Barient single-speed halyard winches is mounted aft on the cabin top edge, one to port and another to starboard. As is common today but was unique for its time, all sail controls are led aft through clutches. The headsail tracks and cars are mounted on the teak-capped toe rails and lead aft to Barient two-speed primary winches and cleats situated on the cockpit coamings. The main is sheeted to a traveler that spans the companionway's threshold.

During its production, the S2 11.0 was offered with a variety of engines including a 32 hp Universal, a 35 hp Volvo Penta, and a 27 hp Yanmar. All are diesels and most all turn a two-blade propeller via a V-drive. A few of the Volvos are connected to sail drives. Access to the engine for routine maintenance is good and is gained from several areas: by removing the companionway stairs and a galley panel, through a panel in the quarter berth, and from inside the port cockpit seat locker. Fuel capacity is 50 gallons.

UNDER WAY

The S2 11.0 is a comfortable, stable, and stiff cruising sailboat. Its displacement of 15,000 pounds makes for easy motion in a seaway. This is confirmed by a motion comfort ratio of 27.4. The boat is by no means fast. However, it is easy to sail and is very forgiving. Its ballast/displacement ratio of 40 percent and capsize screening ratio of 1.95 make it a viable blue-water candidate. It is not a light air performer and its performance decreases the closer it sails to weather. On a run or a broad reach, the boat performs well and exhibits a balanced helm and good tracking.

Under power, the boat is easy to maneuver and will cruise at 6 knots or better.

By the Numbers

Ballast/Displacement Ratio 40%
Displacement/Waterline Length Ratio.......... 297
Sail Area/Displacement Ratio 17.2
Capsize Screening Ratio...................... 1.95
Motion Comfort Ratio 27.4

Things to Check Out

The large fixed portlights are a concern. These should, at the very least, be replaced with thicker material and be fitted with storm shutters. A better bet would be to replace them with a series of much smaller opening portlights. This would not only eliminate a potentially unsafe condition, but if done well, it would also improve the boat's aesthetics.

Having a large cockpit with no bridge deck and a couple of small drains is another potential problem. When offshore, sail with the lower hatch board secured in place and keep a bailer handy. A better solution would be to retrofit a proper bridge deck and enlarge the cockpit drains. Neither project is all that difficult.

Any boat with a balsa-cored deck is a candidate for deck delamination. The S2 11.0 is no exception. One area of chronic leakage is around the chain plates.

While osmotic blistering is not normally a problem, a few boats made early in the production run may exhibit significant damage. The sooner this area is properly addressed, the better.

A few boats were equipped with sail drives. These units are notorious for electrolysis, especially if used in salt water. Epoxy coatings and zincs can help a lot, but a boat with a V-drive is a better bet.

OWNERS' COMMENTS

"...when running she's very confident and responsive...she's strong, stiff, solid, and roomy...I like the sail drive, but I needed to encapsulate the entire housing with marine epoxy to defeat the electrolysis...take her anywhere..." Dan D., 1979 model

"...boat sails well...it has a roomy interior and is well built...I would highly recommend this boat..." Tony T., 1980 model

SUMMING IT UP

The S2 11.0 is a proven cruising yacht that is comfortable, spacious, and easily handled by a short-handed crew. While its sailing performance is middle-of-the-road, it is a forgiving boat and fun to sail. Even though the center cockpit version has a very workable layout, the aft cockpit model is probably better suited for a cruising couple. Built sturdily and finished with care, these boats tend to hold their value. Expect to pay between $35,000 and $55,000.

"Do they ask what pleasure I find at sea?
Why, absence from land is a pleasure to me."

Ralph Waldo Emerson

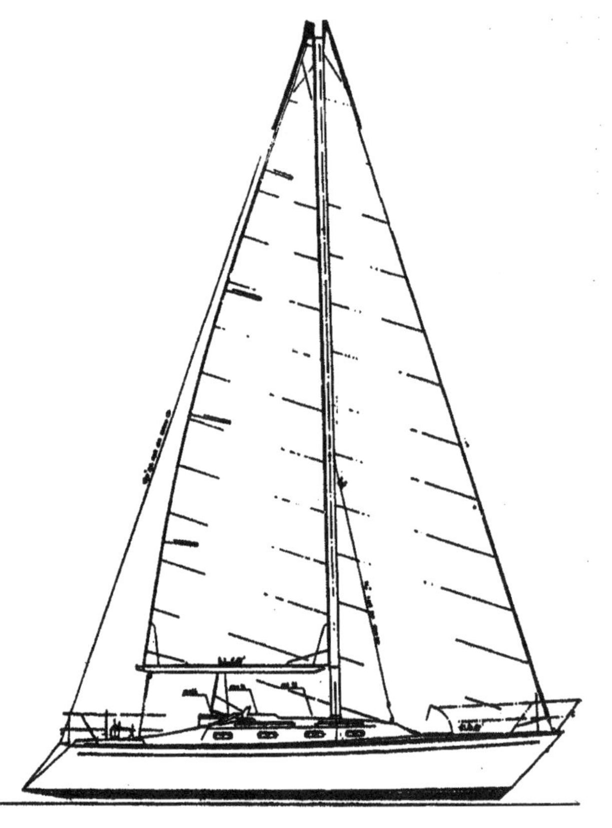

Tartan 34

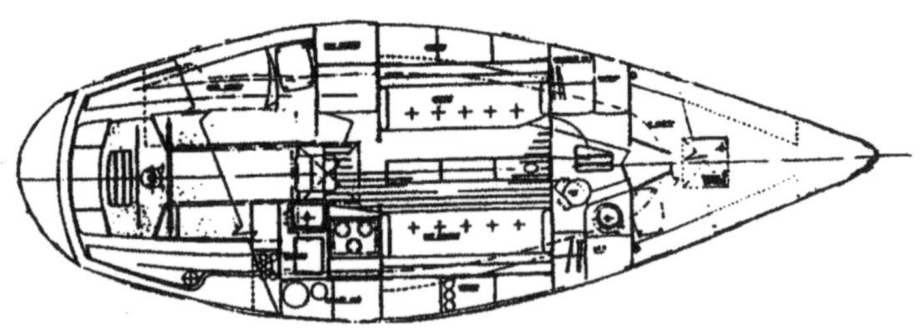

TARTAN 34

A well-engineered and solidly built S&S-designed classic with respectable sailing qualities.

Douglass & McLeod, Inc. of Grand River, Ohio, was the partnership formed by Gordon (Sandy) Douglass and Raymond McLeod Sr. in the late 1940s. It was also the seed organization that has blossomed into what we know today as Tartan Yachts, located across the Grand River in Fairport, Ohio.

Originally, Ray McLeod was a marina owner and builder of wooden commercial fishing boats, while Sandy Douglass was a designer and fabricator of small plywood sailboats, including the Scotsman, the International 14, and the Thistle. Under their combined talents, they introduced the Great Lakes 21 (now known as the International 21) and the Highlander. The partnership lasted about two decades. In 1967, Sandy was bought out and eventually went on to design and build the 19-foot Flying Scot.

In the early 1960s there was considerable interest in the switch to fiberglass. Another company was formed, Douglass and McLeod Plastic Corporation, as well as another partnership, this time with Charlie Britton, an accomplished ocean sailor with financial means. It was Charlie's involvement that led to Douglass and McLeod's switch to auxiliaries. The newly formed company commissioned naval architects Sparkman and Stephens to design the Tartan 27. Not only was the Tartan 27 Douglass and McLeod's first auxiliary, it was Sparkman and Stephens' first design in fiberglass.

The design was so successful that Britton returned to Sparkman and Stephens seeking plans for a 34-footer. Soon after came the Tartan 34, which began a long string of Sparkman and Stephens designs. The development of the Tartan 27 and the Tartan 34 constituted a departure from existing norms of wooden construction to begin a new generation of quality-crafted fiberglass sailboats.

In January 1971 a fire destroyed Douglass and McLeod Plastics, taking with it the molds for the Tartan 34. The following year Ray McLeod Sr. died of cancer. Ray Jr., who had swept the shop floors when he joined the company in 1941, was now part-owner. He soon sold his share of Douglass and McLeod Plastics to Charlie Britton, while retaining ownership of the original company, Douglass and McLeod, Inc. Charlie renamed the company Tartan Marine Corporation and quickly made new molds for the Tartan 34 from a hull and deck an employee had bought to finish himself. The first post-fire boat was hull number 200.

Introduced in 1967, the Tartan 34 was produced until 1978, with a total of 525 boats being built. It was succeeded by the Tartan 37, a boat of exactly the same concept. The Tartan 34 possesses all the attributes of a classic, hence the C one often sees after the 34. This simple designation differentiates between the original version and an updated Tartan 34 that was also a Sparkman and Stephens design introduced in 1985.

DESIGN AND CONSTRUCTION

The Tartan 34's design is a product of the CCA measurement rule and represents the state of the art racer/cruiser for its time. The boat exhibits a springy sheer along with a rakish entry and jaunty stern, on top of which sits a somewhat boxy yet handsome cabin house. While the moderate overhangs produce a short waterline (25 feet) and a displacement/waterline length ratio of 320, add a breeze and the boat's powerful ends will extend the waterline length when it heels. The boat's underbody consists of a long, shallow, swept-back fin keel with centerboard and a skeg-mounted rudder. Olin Stephens, the man who designed this yacht, once said, "There is nothing outstanding or unusual about it. Everything seems to just work well. In a way, it is a masterpiece!"

The construction of the Tartan 34 is quite typical of its day, which had the philosophy that thickness mattered. The hull is heavy and fabricated by hand. It consists of resin-rich alternating laminates of fiberglass mat and woven roving. The deck, also a handlaid laminate, is cored with balsa.

The hull-to-deck joint is somewhat unique. First, an adhesive/sealant was applied to the joint. Then the deck was fastened to the hull by means of stainless steel bolts that were tapped into a strip of aluminum that had been embedded in the inward-facing hull flange. Since no anti-seize compound was used, the resultant hull-to-deck joint is essentially permanent. The teak toe rail was mounted in the same fashion using self-tapping screws.

The 5,000 pounds of lead ballast, encapsulated in the keel, produces a ballast/displacement ratio of 45 percent. The keel also houses the centerboard with its pivot point, positioning cables, and locking mechanism.

The skeg-hung rudder consists of a fiberglass-covered foam core surrounding a carbon steel skeleton that has been welded to a stainless steel rudder post.

The bulkheads are teak-faced and are bonded to the hull. Other surface areas are white or wood-grained plastic laminates trimmed in teak. The cabin sole is unusual in that it is cork. This natural material provides good insulation and traction; however, it tends to hold the dirt and is difficult to clean.

ON DECK

The foredeck of the Tartan 34 is long, narrow, and, except for the necessary mooring cleats and deck pipe, free from obstructions. The side decks are wide and easy to navigate, even with the chain plates situated near their center. The teak handrails along the cabin top are well placed and are within easy reach. A teak toe rail and a nonskid patterned deck make for sure footing.

Situated on the cabin top is a large forward hatch. This is followed by a pair of cowl vents with Dorades flanking the mast. Lastly, a sea hood services the companionway's sliding hatch. The trunk features four forward opening portlights, two per side, and four larger aft fixed portlights, again two per side.

The cockpit, which measures a generous 9 feet 3 inches, features attractive teak coamings. While the coamings may add to the boat's classic looks, crew seated in the cockpit will feel the coamings hit them directly in the small of the back. Outboard of the port and starboard coamings are long, fiberglass winch islands with cubbies beneath. Stowage is in the form of a large starboard cockpit seat locker and a lazarette. There's a substantial bridge deck to keep a flooded cockpit from pouring down below. This is aided by a pair of cockpit drains. Tiller steering was standard equipment; however, many boats also came from the factory with pedestal and wheel. While the tiller leaves the cockpit less cluttered, a forward mounted wheel allows the helmsman to obtain shelter under the dodger.

Original deck hardware is typical of the period. Much of it is chrome-plated bronze. The chrome is likely to be peeling or pitted if the boat has been sailed in salt water. There's a lot of teak on deck, including the toe rail, rubrail, coamings, handrails, and companionway trim. Depending upon the level of maintenance the wood has seen, this can significantly enhance or detract from the boat's appearance.

BELOW DECK

The arrangement of the Tartan 34's accommodations is fairly traditional and functional. It includes good sea berths, well-placed handholds, and a full 6 feet 3 inches of headroom.

The plan includes a 5-foot 11-inch-long V-berth that measures 6 feet 8 inches wide with the filler cushion installed. Centered at the foot of the berth is an upholstered seat, and beneath the berth are stowage bins.

Aft of the V-berth and to starboard is a hanging locker and three-drawer bureau. To port is the head compartment containing all the basic amenities, including a vanity-mounted single stainless steel sink with manual cold water, a marine head, and a locker for stowage. The door to the head doubles as the privacy door for the V-berth.

In the main saloon there are opposing settee/berths, each with built-in leeboards. The starboard berth measures 6 feet 6 inches, the port 6 feet 4 inches. Between the two settees is a bulkhead-mounted drop leaf table. While the starboard settee/berth extends beneath the bureau, the port settee is L-shaped and pulls out to form a double berth. Located beneath the L portion is the engine. Lockers and shelves are situated outboard and above both settee/berths.

Following aft on the starboard side is the L-shaped galley with its pressurized two-burner alcohol cooktop, single stainless steel sink with manual cold water, and a large but marginally insulated icebox. In addition to access from the galley, the icebox has a convenient loading hatch in the starboard cockpit seat. There is an adequate number of shelves, bins, drawers, cubbies, and lockers in which to stow galleyware and provisions. There is even enough room to upgrade to a stove/oven combination without sacrificing too much.

Across from the galley is the forward-facing chart table, followed aft by a generous quarter berth. At almost 7 feet long, the quarter berth makes a good sea berth. As is often the case, the forward portion of the quarter berth doubles as the seat for the chart table.

Most Tartan 34s have a 26-gallon aluminum fuel tank situated under the port settee and a 36-gallon fiberglass potable water tank beneath the starboard settee. Because of the placement of the tanks and the engine, there is no stowage under the settees.

Over the years, Tartan made a few subtle changes to the boat's interior. Wood-grained plastic laminate locker doors were replaced with real wooden louvered door panels. The cork sole was removed and teak-veneered plywood took its place. Also, a pilot berth with drawers beneath replaced the port outboard lockers and shelves.

SPECIFICATIONS

LOA .... 34'5"
LWL .... 25'
Beam .... 10'2"
Draft .... (board up/down) 3'11"/8'4"
Displacement .... 11,200 lbs.
Ballast .... 5,000 lbs.
Sail Area .... 483 sq. ft.

THE RIG

With a single pair of spreaders, a single pair of cap shrouds, and double lowers, the Tartan 34's rig is about as simple and sturdy as one can get. Both spars of this masthead sloop are anodized aluminum extrusions with internal sail tracks. The keel-stepped mast has a bridge clearance of 44 feet 10 inches. And the boom came standard with roller reefing. The original sail area totaled 527 square feet. In the early 1970s, to make the boat rate better under the emerging IOR, the boom was shortened by about 2½ feet. This eliminated 54 square feet of sail area, which didn't help the Tartan 34's light air performance. While the smaller mainsail area significantly reduced weather helm, neither the base of the headsail nor the height of the rig was increased to offset this loss of sail area.

Originally, the mainsheet was led aft to a traveler that bisected the cockpit just aft of the tiller. While this cumbersome arrangement crowded the helmsman and broke up the cockpit, it was necessary because of the old-fashioned roller-reefing boom. With the shorter boom (still equipped with roller reefing), the traveler was relocated to a better spot, just aft of the bridge deck.

Other sail-handling gear includes a pair of Barient #10 mast-mounted halyard winches, a single #10 for mainsheet control, and a pair of Barient #21 two-speed primaries, mounted on the port and starboard winch islands.

The Tartan 34's original engine was the ubiquitous Atomic 4. Around 1975, the Farymann R-30-M diesel was offered as an option. Since the Atomic 4 was a smoother running and quieter engine, the Farymann never became popular. Either engine is adequate. Engine access beneath the L-shaped settee is excellent.

UNDER WAY

Among the primary reasons that the Tartan 34 is considered a classic are its sailing characteristics. Like most Sparkman and Stephens' designs, the Tartan 34 handles well in a variety of conditions. And it doesn't possess any significant bad habits.

While the boat sails well to weather, the Tartan 34, like most centerboarders, really shines off the wind where it is most efficient. On a run, its optimum jib angle is 173 degrees, which is deeper than many modern fin-keeled boats.

Like most other boats, the Tartan 34 likes to be sailed on its feet. It is initially tender, but when the wind pipes up the boat stiffens up. These conditions are reflected in the boat's motion comfort ratio of 28.13 and its 1.82 capsize screening ratio. At a heel angle of over 20 degrees, the boat tends to slow down and make leeway. Take the first reef in at around 15 knots and a second tuck just over 20 knots. Also, by keeping the centerboard down, weather helm can be reduced.

Coupled to the standard two-bladed propeller, the Atomic 4 supplies a cruising speed of 6 knots, despite the fact that the propeller is partially hidden behind the trailing edge of the keel, which reduces prop efficiency. Also, because the propeller is so far forward, backing down in a straight line is difficult.

BY THE NUMBERS

Ballast/Displacement Ratio	45%
Displacement/Waterline Length Ratio	.320
Sail Area/Displacement Ratio	15.44
Capsize Screening Ratio	1.82
Motion Comfort Ratio	28.13

THINGS TO CHECK OUT

For all of its fine attributes, the Tartan 34 is not without its shortcomings. The centerboard's lifting, pivoting, and locking mechanisms should be routinely checked for wear. Since the centerboard can be locked in various positions of depth, it lacks the ability to be kicked up in the event of a grounding. This is an area that should be looked at when the boat is on the hard.

Delamination of the boat's balsa-cored deck is another common problem. Areas especially prone to damage include around all through-bolted fittings, especially the stanchions and chain plates. The bulkheads and glassed-in knees to which the chain plates are bolted should be carefully inspected for rot. The forward edge of the cabin trunk where it meets the deck is prone to significant gelcoat cracking and crazing and subsequent delamination.

Water saturating the foam-cored rudder is also common. In severe cases, the weld connecting the mild steel skeleton to the stainless steel rudder post corrodes. This allows the rudder post to turn independently of the rudder.

Originally, the through-hulls of the Tartan 34 were nothing more than brass pipe nipples that were glassed into the hull, with gate valves on the inside. While this may be marginally acceptable for fresh water use, in salt water, galvanic corrosion will quickly take its toll. If not already done, these should be replaced with proper through-hull fittings and seacocks.

Other areas that are deficient include the undersized cockpit drains and their rigid pipe connections, the icebox with its minimal insulation, and the boat's rudimentary electrical system.

OWNERS' COMMENTS

"...lovely S&S design with great sailing qualities...sails well in all but the lightest air...has enough to her to punch through a good chop and headwind..." BJ L., 1972 model

"...no serious bad habits...just trim the sails and adjust the board and you can lock the helm and she will sail herself...engine location is near the center of gravity and access is extremely good...good sailing boat that is well built..." Peter C., 1974 model

"...sea-kindly, great sailing boat...sails better, in many respects, than many newer designs..." Jim M., 1975 model

SUMMING IT UP

The Tartan 34 is a well-designed, well-built, easily managed sailboat. As it originally came, the boat is old-fashioned by today's standards and is not without its deficiencies. If one is willing to spend the time and money to address these deficiencies plus make some minor upgrades, the boat is worth it and is suited for offshore cruising. Tartan 34s can be found all over the world. Expect to pay between $20,000 and $32,000.

> "To my mind, the greatest joy in yachting
> is to cruise along some lovely coast,
> finding one's way into all sorts of
> out-of-the-way coves and rivers."
>
> R.D. Graham

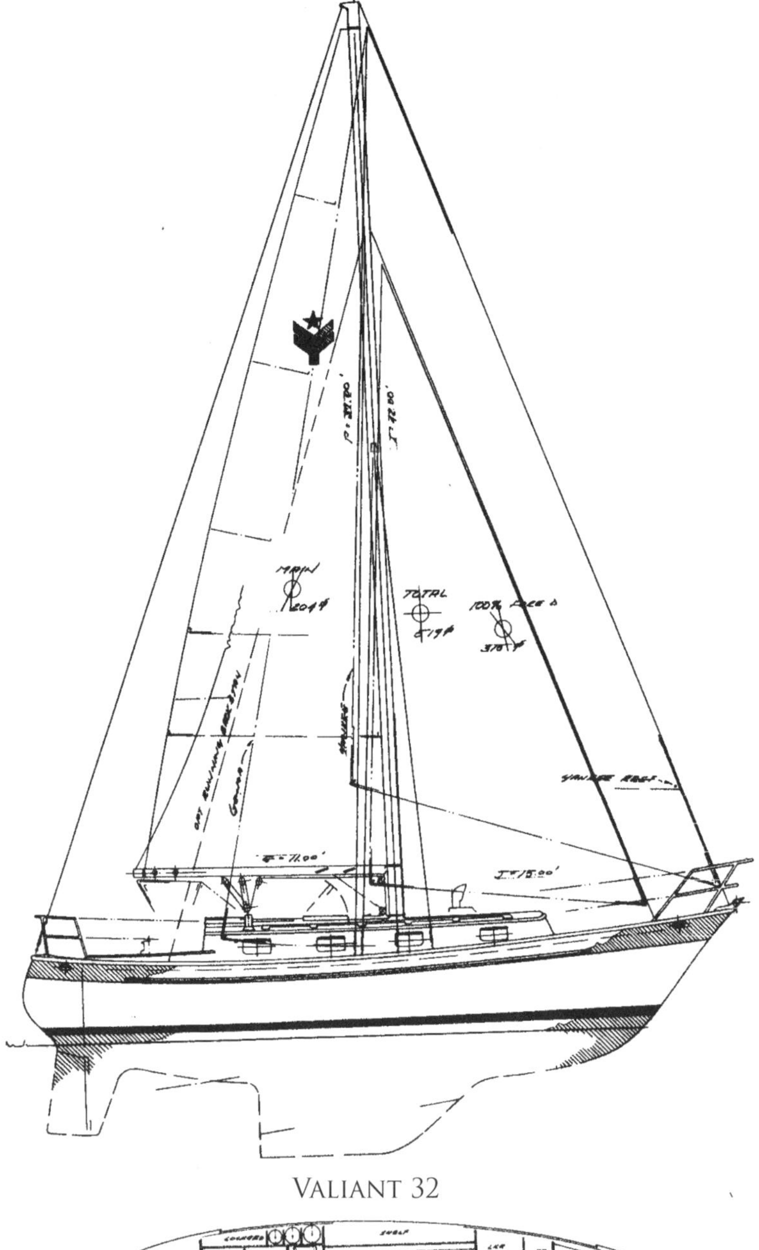

VALIANT 32

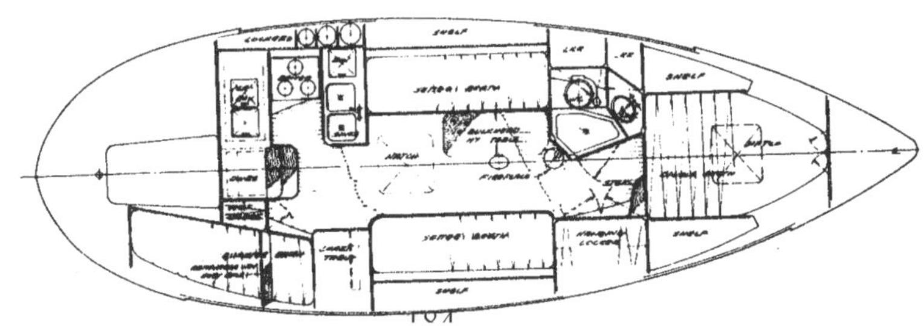

Valiant 32

A yacht conceived as an offshore vessel.

The seed of what was to eventually blossom out as Valiant Yachts began its germination in a Seattle, Washington spaghetti house. Here a group of young, idealistic, and enthusiastic people came together with a lot of creative energy and developed the concept for a new class of cruising sailboat. Stan and Sylvia Dabney, Nathan Rothman, and a young designer named Robert Perry had no idea that this new and "radical" boat would become something special.

Valiant Yacht's concept, not an actual boat, was introduced at the 1975 Miami Boat Show. Some interest was developed and the Valiant contingent returned to Seattle with orders for three, possibly four, boats. Uniflite of Bellingham, Washington was contracted to build 12 hulls for this new 40-footer. Located 90 miles north of Seattle, Uniflite was a powerboat and one-time sailboat manufacturer.

The Valiant 40 was an instant success. By the time the first boat was launched, the fledgling company had orders for eight boats. More orders followed, and by 1978, the company was building and selling some 50 boats a year, including the Valiant 40 and the Valiant 32.

A gentleman by the name of Dane Nelson often visited the Valiant office in Seattle and repeatedly asked that they build a boat with a pilothouse. Stan Dabney's tongue-in-cheek response was always, "It will never happen unless you buy the company." Dane, along with his partner Sam Dick, eventually did just that. Around 1982 or so, after building 10 pilothouse

Valiants, they sold the company to Uniflite, which later became Chris Craft. The new owners, not wanting to continue in the sailboat business, sold the Valiant name and mold inventory to Rich Worstell, a successful Valiant dealer. For a short time Rich continued production in Seattle; then, in 1985, he relocated the company to its current location just outside of Houston, in Gordenville, Texas.

The Valiant 32 was designed in the wake of the Valiant 40's success. It wasn't merely a smaller version of the Valiant 40, but was in fact built in response to a demand for a 30- to 35-foot couple's cruising boat. And according to Bob Perry, it was designed to do everything better than the Valiant 40. The yacht was not merely to be *capable* of offshore passages, but was intended to perform as an offshore vessel. Introduced in 1977 and remaining in production through the mid '80s, a total of 67 Valiant 32s were produced.

Design and Construction

The lines of the Valiant 32 are very traditional and incorporate a moderate sheer, a fairly sharp and relatively deep entry, and a full stern. There is a slight degree of flair at the bow. This feature is responsible for a dry ride when on the wind and the boat's refusal to take green water over the bow. The canoe-shaped stern is not only aesthetically pleasing, but is extremely effective in a following sea. The underbody, with its moderate deadrise, features a modified fin keel with external lead ballast, a small bustle, and a skeg-mounted rudder.

The one-piece hull is handlaid fiberglass in a solid matrix of alternating layers of woven roving and mat wet out with polyester resin. The deck and cabin top laminates are cored with end-grain balsa. Somewhere in the late 1970s, the boat was built with a polyester resin that contained a fire retardant additive. Over time, this additive caused severe blistering. Since the blistering came from within the laminate, the entire boat was affected, not just its bottom. The fire retardant additive was dropped in the early 1980s.

ON DECK

The deck plan of the Valiant 32 is straightforward and quite workable. The broad foredeck's most prominent feature is the boat's large forward hatch. Good footing and maneuvering is provided by the molded-in nonskid deck surface, and augmented by teak-capped bulwarks and a stainless steel bow pulpit. The side decks are comfortably wide.

The forward portion of the cabin exhibits the traditional turtle-shell shape. On its top is a pair of forward cowl ventilators with Dorades, a large hatch over the main saloon, and a proper sea hood. Also within easy reach is a pair of cabin-length teak handrails. Situated on each side of the cabin trunk are four equally-sized opening portlights.

Perhaps the most notable feature of the Valiant 32 is its comfortable cockpit. The high, sloped, teak-capped cockpit coamings afford good back support. There is a minimum of three cockpit seat lockers (one to port and a pair flanking the helmsman). Add a fourth starboard locker if the boat is configured without a quarter berth. A pair of cockpit drains along with a bridge deck keep water from cascading below. Other features include tiller steering or wheel steering via cable/quadrant, a stern anchor roller and deck pipe, a stainless steel stern pulpit, and a transom-mounted swim ladder. Visibility over the long cabin is excellent.

BELOW DECK

The traditional Valiant interior consists of a large V-berth forward with access to both the chain locker in the forepeak and the port and starboard potable water tanks beneath. The foredeck hatch provides natural illumination and ventilation, complemented by a trio of 12-volt lamps and a two-speed fan.

Aft and to starboard is a large hanging locker and a series of shelves, above which are an opening portlight and a cowl ventilator. On the port side is the head compartment, featuring a vanity-mounted single stainless steel sink with both pressurized hot and cold water and a manual foot pump; a shower with separate sump; a marine head; and outboard stowage. An opening portlight and cowl ventilator service this compartment. The door to the head swings aft and latches to the hanging locker. This gives privacy to the V-berth and the small area immediately aft.

Amidships is the main saloon with its opposing settees and centerline drop leaf table. The starboard settee/berth has stowage above, outboard, and below, plus it is fitted with a lee cloth. The port settee pulls out and converts to a small double. It, too, features stowage above, outboard, and below, plus a lee cloth. Overhead are a large hatch, a pair of handrails, a dome light, and four opening portlights.

The U-shaped galley is aft and to port. Standard amenities include a gimbaled stove, a large icebox in the aft counter, and in-the-counter dry stowage lockers. There's also a dual stainless steel sink with hot and cold pressurized water, as well as a manual foot pump for potable water. Potable water capacity is approximately 80 gallons. There's an opening portlight, the companionway hatch, and a dome light in this area.

Across from the galley is the forward-facing navigation station. The chart table is sized to accommodate chart books or folded charts. Beneath the table top there is adequate stowage for navigation gear plus rolled charts. There are also stowage lockers outboard and beneath the navigation station's seat. The seat is quite comfortable and has good head clearance. An opening portlight plus a dome light and a flexible chart lamp service this area.

The Valiant 32 offered two interior options for the space just aft of the navigation station. One option featured an enclosed quarter berth cabin with a double quarter berth and a hanging locker. This configuration pushed the starboard settee/berth forward and reduced the size of the forward hanging locker. The other option eliminated the quarter berth and in its place gave a cavernous stowage area. With this arrangement, the starboard settee/berth aligned with the port settee/berth, resulting in a larger forward hanging locker. Both options incorporate a handy wet locker within one step of the companionway.

The interior is oiled teak throughout and headroom is a generous 6 feet 4 inches. The overhead panels are a white laminate with teak battens, while the cabin sole is fiberglass with a molded-in nonskid pattern plus teak hatches and gratings.

SPECIFICATIONS

LOA .... 32'
LWL .... 26'
Beam .... 10'5"
Draft .... (deep/shoal) 5'2"/4'6"
Displacement .... 11,800 lbs.
Ballast .... 4,700 lbs.
Sail Area .... 524 sq. ft.

THE RIG

With a displacement/waterline length ratio of nearly 300, the Valiant 32 is a moderate displacement boat. Most boats are cutter rigged. This breaks the sail area down into an easily managed sail plan. The keel-stepped mast is situated somewhat aft to accommodate the inner forestay. Both spars are aluminum extrusions with internal sail tracks. Bridge clearance is 49 feet, 9 inches. The standing rigging consists of a headstay, inner forestay, a pair of cap shrouds, dual lower shrouds, a single backstay, and a pair of intermediate backstays.

All halyards are cleated at the mast; mechanical advantage is obtained through the use of a pair of mast-mounted Barient winches. The headsail sheets are led through cars and tracks situated on the side decks and terminated at Barient primaries located on the teak-topped cockpit coamings. The staysail tracks, on the cabin top, lead the sheets to a pair of cabin-top winches. The main traveler is located on the cabin top and spans the companionway's sliding hatch.

Most Valiant 32s are equipped with a 25 hp Westerbeke diesel connected to a two-blade bronze propeller via a V-drive. A few boats, maybe six or seven, were fitted with a 24 hp Universal diesel. Either power plant is sufficient. Fuel capacity is 40 gallons and access to the engine is rated as fair.

UNDER WAY

The Valiant 32 is a dry boat. It sails best when on its feet. Keep the teak rubrail, which is located about ten inches below the caprail, out of the water for the best performance. With the mast stepped aft to accommodate the inner forestay, the boat tends to develop weather helm when the winds exceed 15 knots. Reefing early balances out the boat nicely. A few boats were sloop-rigged with their masts stepped farther forward. This reduced weather helm and simplified sail controls. Overall, the boat's endearing qualities include windward performance, excellent maneuverability, and generally a light helm. The canoe-shaped stern is extremely effective in a following sea. Its motion comfort ratio is 28.13 and its capsize screening ratio is 1.83.

The 4-cylinder Westerbeke engine consumes approximately ½ gallon of fuel per hour at hull speed, which equates to a 500-mile cruising range when under power.

BY THE NUMBERS

Ballast/Displacement Ratio 40%
Displacement/Waterline Length Ratio....... 299.72
Sail Area/Displacement Ratio 16.18
Capsize Screening Ratio..................... 1.83
Motion Comfort Ratio 28.71

THINGS TO CHECK OUT

Along with all the typical age-related problems, there are two areas of significant concern: delamination of the balsa cored deck and severe blistering.

While a balsa-cored deck is extremely light and adds structural rigidity, constant flexing of the cored deck can cause a break in the bond between the two fiberglass layers and the balsa core. Also, any water that might find its way beneath the fiberglass skin can turn the core to mush. Check around all through-bolted deck fittings for proper bedding. Also sound out the deck.

The blistering is not osmotic blistering caused by water penetrating the gelcoat from outside and setting up a chemical reaction in the laminate, but rather is the result of a fire retardant additive that did not completely react with the polyester resin. This problem comes from within. The unreacted fire retardant slowly wicks its way through the laminate to the surface and forms blisters. These blisters will show up over the entire boat, not just on the bottom. They seem to be more evident in warm climates and in areas where the laminate is the warmest. Boats sailed in cold waters are very slow to develop blisters. Fortunately, not all Valiant 32s suffer from this form of blistering. Only boats that were built in the late 1970s and early 1980s were affected. The fire retardant additive was dropped in the early 1980s. Properly addressing this form of blistering is labor-intensive and can be costly.

OWNERS' COMMENTS

" ...one of the best values for a small blue-water boat...have lived aboard since 1997...handles extremely well in heavy weather..." Justin W., 1977 model

"...very strongly built...one of the fire retardant blistered boats...I have done all repairs myself...very satisfied...built to go anywhere..." Norman R., 1978 model

"...sailed to New Zealand and back...strong, well-behaved boat...a blister factory though easy to keep under control...strongly recommend..." Joel T., 1978 model

SUMMING IT UP

The Valiant 32 is an easily handled yacht. It is near ideal for the cruising couple. The fin keel and skeg-mounted rudder make the boat fast and responsive, the canoe stern is excellent in a confused or following sea, and the high forward bulwarks and flared bow keep it dry and comfortable. Below, the accommodations are pleasant, functional, and roomy. Despite the fact that earlier models were prone to blistering, prices have remained fairly uniform. Expect to pay around $55,000 for a boat in sail-away condition.

"The object of cruising is to make a complete change of surroundings,
a change for the eyes, ears, and nose...
a cabin should be very different from a city apartment...
you should not lug along what you are trying to leave behind."

L. Francis Herreshoff

Appendix A

Ballast/Displacement Ratio (B/D)
Displacement/Waterline Length Ratio (D/L)
Sail Area/Displacement Ratio (SA/D)
Capsize Screening Factor (CSF)
Motion Comfort Ratio (CR)

BALLAST/DISPLACEMENT RATIO (B/D)

(Ballast/Displacement) x 100

The B/D ratio is achieved by dividing the ballast by the total displacement. The value can be expressed as either a decimal or a percentage (if multiplied by 100). The ratio shows what portion of the total displacement is in the form of ballast and can be an indicator of a particular boat's "stiffness" or "tenderness."

This value should be used with care. The placement of the ballast and the boat's hull shape each play a very important role. For example, one boat may have a deep keel with its ballast located at the bottom, while another boat is fitted with a shoal draft keel with the ballast located closer to the boat's hull. The two boats will have identical B/D ratios. However, they more than likely will have very different "righting moments," which is what actually determines the "stiffness" or "tenderness" of the boat.

On a boat, the center of gravity (CG) is a fixed point. Its location is determined by the way in which the boat has been constructed and loaded. The center of buoyancy (CB), on the other hand, shifts sideways as the boat heels or rolls. When at rest, a boat's CG and CB are aligned vertically. As the boat heels or rolls, the weight of the boat acts downward at the CG and the buoyant force of the water acts upward at the CB. As a result, these forces create a rotating motion called the righting moment.

Some boat manufacturers who offer both shoal and deep keel versions of the same boats (*e.g.* Catalina, O'day) routinely increase the amount of ballast in their shoal keel versions. The intention here is to help maintain similar righting moments between the two versions. Often this works. However, when it doesn't, the shoal draft boat with the higher B/D ratio will exhibit a lower righting moment and be less "stiff" than the deep keel version.

DISPLACEMENT/WATERLINE LENGTH RATIO (D/L)

(Displacement/2240)/([Waterline x 0.01]^3)

The D/L ratio is a nondimensional value that is derived by dividing the displacement, in long tons, by 0.01 waterline cubed. It is the most widely used value when comparing boats, and indicates whether a boat is of "heavy" or "light" displacement for its length. The following table lists various D/L ratios and boat types generally associated with them:

Boat Type	D/L Ratio
Light racing multi-hull	40-50
Ultra-light ocean racer	60-100
Very light ocean racer	100-150
Light cruiser/racer	150-200
Light cruising auxiliary	200-250
Average cruising auxiliary	250-300
Heavy cruising auxiliary	300-350
Very heavy cruising auxiliary	350-400

Because the D/L ratio is nondimensional (i.e. achieved using a cube of the waterline length), it can be used to compare the displacement of boats of widely different waterline lengths.

Generally a boat displaying a lower D/L ratio will exhibit better light air performance for a given sail area than a boat with a higher D/L ratio. Further, the boat with the lower D/L ratio will be more sensitive to loading, will likely need to shorten sail sooner, and will probably afford a less comfortable ride in challenging sea conditions.

A boat exhibiting a higher D/L ratio will be less affected by loading, have a slower motion in a seaway, will need more sail in light air, and may sail wet.

SAIL AREA/DISPLACEMENT RATIO (SA/D)

Sail Area with 100% Foresail/ ([Displacement/64]^2/3)

The SA/D ratio is obtained by dividing the sail area by the displacement in cubic feet to the 2/3 power. It is a nondimensional "power to weight" ratio that can be used to compare the relative "horsepower" of boats of different sizes. The follow table lists various SA/D ratios and general boat types:

SA/D RATIO	BOAT TYPE
< 14	heavy cruisers and motorsailers
17-17	ocean cruisers
18-18	coastal cruisers
20-20	racing dinghies, inshore racers, ocean racing yachts
>20	high-performance racers

A boat with a high SA/D ratio will accelerate better and will perform better in light air. It will reach hull speed with less wind and will need to have its sails shortened sooner to avoid being over-canvassed.

Conversely, a boat with a low SA/D will exhibit lackluster light air performance and may rely more heavily on its auxiliary engine during these conditions.

CAPSIZE SCREENING FACTOR (CSF)

The CSF ratio is obtained by dividing the maximum beam by the cube root of the displacement in cubic feet. To convert the displacement from pounds to cubic feet, divide by 64.

The CSF ratio was developed by the Cruising Club of America and estimates a boat's resistance to capsizing. It compares beam with displacement, since excess beam contributes to capsizing and heavy displacement reduces the vulnerability to capsizing. In general, heavy boats with narrow hulls are more stable.

The CSF ratio serves only as a guide. A boat is an acceptable blue water candidate if the CSF ratio is 2.0 or less. The lower the better.

The CSF ratio does not take into account the vertical position of the boat's center of gravity (VCG). The VCG is a contributing factor when studying a boat's vulnerability to capsizing. Generally, the lower the better. The VCG can be lowered by a longer keel or by having more ballast at the end of the keel. Should capsizing occur, a low VCG will greatly help in self-righting the boat.

MOTION COMFORT RATIO (CR)

Displacement/(2/3 x [(7/10 x LWL)+(1/3 x LOA)] x Beam^4/3)

The CR ratio was developed by Ted Brewer, one of North America's best-known yacht designers. It is based on the fact that the faster the motion, the more uncomfortable the passengers. At a given wave height, the speed of the boat's upward motion is dependent upon the boat's displacement and the amount of waterline that is acted upon. The greater the displacement or the lesser the waterline area, the slower the motion and the more comfort for a given sea state.

The CR ratio predicts the overall comfort of a boat when under way. Ratios can vary from 5.0 (a light daysailer) to the high 60s (very heavy ocean vessel). Ocean cruisers generally exhibit a CR in the 30s.

Higher values denote a more comfortable ride. With an increase in displacement, the CR ratio will increase. As the length and, to a lesser extent, the beam increases, the CR ratio will decrease.

Keep in mind that a yacht heeled by a good breeze will have a much steadier motion than one bobbing up and down in light air on leftover swells from yesterday's storm.

Appendix B

Owners' Associations

OWNERS' ASSOCIATIONS

Alberg 35 User Group
Tom Alley
38 Woodland Dr
Big Flats, NY 14814
Phone: 607-562-3909
http://www.alberg35.org

Alberg 35
www.pce.net/alley/alberg35.html

Allied Luders 33 Owners' Association
Allen Gamache
One Shenandoah Drive
Paxton, MA 01612-1015
http://www.geocities.com/timessquare/arcade/9282/index.html

Allied Princess 36
Todd Dunn
P.O. Box 52
Bass Harbor, ME 04653
Phone: 207-244-3471
http://www.geocities.com/TheTropics/8005/AP36PAGE.html

Baba, Panda, Tashiba
Richard B. Emerson
PO Box 1628
Skippack, PA 19474-1628
http://www.geocities.com/babaweb1/home.htm http://sail2live.com/boats/showcase

Baba 30
www.baba30.com

Bayfield Yacht Owner Resources
Peter Haliburton
http://www.geocities.com/bayfieldyachts

Bayfield Yachts Owners Group
Mark Topping
http://www.bayfieldyachtowners.org

Bristol Owners' Association
Douglas Axtell
http://hometown.aol.com/bristolyht/index.html

C&C
http://www.cncphotoalbum.com/

Cape Dory Sailboat Owners Association
www.capedory.org/cdinfo.html

Cheoy Lee
James and Cilla McGarvey
PO Box 42
South Plymouth, NY 13844
http://www.cheoyleeassociation.com

CSY (Caribbean Sailing Yachts)
Dave Covert
to subscribe: majordomo@List-Server.net

Endeavour Owners' Forum
Paul Uhl
1828 Asbury Avenue
Evanston, IL 60201-3504
http://www.endeavourowners.com

Island Packet 31 Owners' Association
Jonathan Bickel
P.O. Box 1216
Ocean Springs, MS 39566
Phone: 228-522-0120
Phone: 228-249-1080
http://www.ip31ownersassoc.homestead.com
(Web address is a discussion group.)

Islander Owners Association
http://www.islandersailboats.com

Islander Sailboats
www.**sailboat**owners.com/forums/menunew.tpl?fno=423

Morgan 38 Owners' Group
Alan and Sheri Tigner
18 N Chestnut Ct
Hawthorn Woods, IL 60047
Phone: 847-402-4315 (daytime)
Phone: 847-550-0381 (home)

Niagara 35
http://members.rogers.com/n35/index.html

Pacific Seacraft
http://www.pacificseacraft.com

Pearson 35 Site
Ron Lambert
http://www.geocities.com/Eureka/6028

Pearson 35
www.pearson35.com/linkspage

Tartan 34 Owners Association
Deane Holt
http://t34.tartanowners.org

S2 Yachts
http://www.anglefire.com/mi/loosecruise/S2/index.html

Valiant Yachts Owners' Association
Sylvia and Stanley Dabney
255 East 22nd Court
Riviera Beach, FL 33404
Phone: 561-845-9303
Fax: 561-845-9304
http://www.offshoreyachts.com

APPENDIX C

Comparison Spreadsheet

Boat	LOA	LWL	Beam	Displacement (pounds)	Ballast (pounds)	Draft	Sail Ar (sq. ft
Alberg 35	34'9"	24'	9'8"	12,600	5,300	5'2"	545sl/5
Allied Princess 36	36	27'6"	11'	14,400	5,000	4'6"	595sl/8
Baba 30	34'6"	24'6"	10'3"	12,500	4,000	4'9"	504
Bayfield 32	32'	23'3"	10'6"	9,600	4,000	3'9"	525
Bristol 35.5	35'6"	27'6"	10'10"	15,000	6,500d 7,000cb	5'9"d 3'9"-9'6"cb	589
C&C Landfall 35	34'11"	26'9"	10'8"	13,000	5,500	4'10"	545
Cape Dory 33	33'1/2"	24'6"	10'3"	13,300	5,500	4'10"	539sl/5
Chcoy Lee Clipper 36	35'7"	25'	10'9"	16,250	5,375	5'3"	635
CSY 37	37'3"	29'2"	12'	19,689	8,000	6'2"d/4'8"sh	610
Endeavour 37	37'5"	30'	11'7"	21,000	8,000	4'6"	580sl/6
Islander 32 MK II	31'11½"	25'	11'1"	10,500	4,200	5'4"d/4'sh	523
Island Packet 31	34'4"	S2	11'6"	11,000	4,500	4'd/3'-7'cb	531
Luders 33	33'1"	24'	10'	12,800	4,500	5'	574
Morgan 382	38'4"	30'6"	12'	17,000	6,800	6'd/5'sh	668
Niagara 35	35'1"	26'8"	11'5"	14,000	5,500	5'2"	598
Pacific Seacraft 31	31'10"	24'2"	9'10"	11,000	4,400	4'11"d/4'sh	485sl/6
Pearson 35	35'	25'	10'	13,000	5,400	3'9"-7'6"	550
S2 11.0 (aft)	36'	28'3"	11'11"	15,000	6,000	5'6"d/4'8"sh	632
Tartan 34	34'5"	25'	10'2"	11,200	5,000	3'11"-8'4"	483
Valiant 32	32'	26'	10'5"	11,800	4,700	5'2"d/4'6"sh	524

KEY:

c=cutter
cb=centerboard
d=deep
k=ketch
sh=shoal
sl=sloop
y=yawl

B/D	D/L	SA/D	CSF	CR	LOD	Fuel (gallons)	Water (gallons)
42	406.9	16.1sl/17.23y	1.66	34.59		23	48
35	309.11	16.08sl/16.33k	1.81	30.16		40	80
32	379.46	14.97	1.77	33.15	29'9"	35	80
42	330.23	18.6	1.98	24.68		20	20
43d 47cb	321.99	15.49	1.76	32.2		31	100
42	303.2	15.77	1.82	29.18		40	64
41	403.74	15.36sl/15.6c	1.73	33.98		21	84
33	464.29	15.84	1.7	37.43		60	100
41	354.13	13.39	1.78	34.93		50	120
38	347.22	12.19sl/13.45k	1.68	38.3		55	100
40	300	17.45	2.02	24.16		30	52
41	229.8	17.18	2.07	22.81	30'7"	25	60
35	413.36	16.78	1.71	34.23		25	50
40	267.49	16.49	1.87	29.01		40	55
39	329.47	16.47	1.9	28.71		30	80
40	348.22	15.69sl/19.41c	1.77	30.81	30'6"	23	65
42	371.43	15.92	1.7	33.18		20	80
40	297	17.2	1.95	27.4		50	80
45	320	15.44	1.82	28.13		26	36
40	299.72	16.18	1.83	28.71		40	80

Bibliography

Brewer, Ted. *Ted Brewer Explains Sailboat Design.* Camden, ME: International Marine, 1984.

Brewer, Ted. *Understanding Boat Design.* Fourth Edition. Camden ME: International Marine, 1994.

Casey, Don and Hackler, Lew. *Sensible Cruising: The Thoreau Approach.* Camden, ME: International Marine, 1986.

Dodds, Don. *Modern Cruising Under Sail.* New York: The Lyons Press, 1998.

Du Plessis, Hugo. *Fiberglass Boats.* Second Edition. London: Adlard Coles Limited, 1973.

Gustafson, Charles. *How to Buy the Best Sailboat.* Revised Edition. New York: Hearst Marine Books, 1991.

Kinney, Francis S. *Skene's Elements of Yacht Design.* Eighth Edition. New York: Dodd, Mead & Co., 1981.

Kirschenbaum, Jerome & Harris, Brayton. *Safe Boat.* New York: W.W. Norton & Co., 1990.

Myatt, John. *Effective Skippering.* Dobbs Ferry, NY: Sheridan House, 1992.

Naranjo, Ralph J. *Wind Shadow West.* New York: Hearst Marine Books, 1983.

Neale, Tom. *All in the Same Boat.* Camden, ME: International Marine, 1997.

Pardey, Lin & Larry. *The Capable Cruiser.* Arcata, CA: Paradise Cay Publishing, 1987.

Pardey, Lin & Larry. *The Self-Sufficient Sailor.* Revised Edition. Arcata, CA: Paradise Cay Publishing, 1997.

Spurr, Daniel. *Upgrading the Cruising Sailboat,* Newport, Rhode Island: Seven Seas Press, Inc., 1983.

ABOUT THE AUTHOR

Gregg Nestor has had a lifelong interest in all things aquatic since his early childhood on the southern shore of Lake Erie. In 1979, Gregg stepped aboard a sailboat for the first time; so began one of his life's great passions... sailing. His cruising has taken him along the Atlantic seaboard, the Gulf of Mexico, and the Caribbean. He performs much of his own maintenance and upgrades and has developed several novel approaches to common sailing dilemmas.

Gregg has written numerous articles, which have been featured in several sailing magazines, including *Sailing, Latitudes and Attitudes, Small Craft Advisor*, and *Good Old Boat*, where he is a contributing editor. His first book, *All Hands On Deck: Become Part of a Caribbean Sailing Adventure* (AuthorHouse) is a children's book that even adults will want in their libraries.

When not writing about sailing or tending to chores on the family farm, Gregg and his wife Joyce can be found cruising the Great Lakes aboard *Raconteur*, their Pearson 28-2.